The Great Sex Divide

The Great Sex Divide

· A Study of Male–Female Differences

Glenn Wilson

Peter Owen · London

ISBN 0 7206 0750 7

PETER OWEN PUBLISHERS
73 Kenway Road London SW5 0RE

First published in Great Britain 1989
© Glenn Wilson 1989

Printed in Great Britain by WBC Print Bristol and Maesteg

Contents

1 · *Sex and Evolution*

A certain professor of philosophy once dreamed that he had discovered the secret of the universe. Waking momentarily, he jotted it down on his bedside pad and resumed his slumber. In the morning he remembered the experience and excitedly snatched his pad to see what it said. It read: 'Higgamus hoggamus, women are monogamous; hoggamus higgamus, men are polygamous.' The professor was greatly disappointed, for while he thought it was probably true, he doubted that it was any secret, let alone the 'secret of the universe'. In this book, I shall argue that it is a very important truth and one that many people have lost sight of because of wishful thinking and the application of political blinkers.

If I were to say 'Men are taller than women', there would be probably be little protest. This is patently true *as a generalization*, even though there are many exceptions to the rule; particular men are shorter than particular women. People can accept that height is a characteristic which is objectively and reliably measured, so that the extent of separation and overlap in the height distribution of men and women may be easily determined. Then, if I were to raise the question as to how this difference arose, few people would look to an environmental explanation. Although it might be possible to argue that in our chauvinistic society men gain for themselves more nourishing food than women, thus enabling them to grow up taller, this theory would seldom be seriously advanced even by feminists. In fact, there is fairly widespread agreement that the difference has come about as a result of evolutionary processes. Male animals have become specialized as hunters and fighters, while the females have developed attributes that equip them for motherhood.

However, when I say that 'men are more sexually exploratory in nature than women', the suggestion is often greeted by howls of disbelief and even rage. Some women deny that there is any such difference between men and women, perhaps citing their own exceptional libido or that of their friends as evidence. Others admit the generalization is true but claim that it has come about because men and women have been 'taught by our society' to think, feel and behave in different ways.

Among the other sundry and sometimes inconsistent objections that are heard to echo about an auditorium are: 'How can you possibly measure something like a sex drive?'; 'That only applies to our society at the moment, lots of other cultures are different'; 'That may have been so in the past, but hasn't the difference largely disappeared since the advent of contraception and women's liberation?'; 'By saying that you only reinforce the stereotype and make it all the more difficult for us to change it.' One other objection, which is more often voiced by males, is 'Why bother to make the point? It is so self-evident.'

Clearly, there are a number of separate questions here that need to be dealt with independently.

1 What is the nature and extent of the difference between men and women?
2 If the difference exists, what is its origin or cause?
3 How easily could the difference be dismantled, if this were agreed upon as a desirable end?

I shall tackle these different questions in turn.

Attitudes towards love and sex

One of the most striking differences in mentality between women and men is illustrated by a snippet from one of Woody Allen's films. 'Sex without love is an empty experience,' posits Diane Keaton. 'Yes,' replies Allen, 'but as empty experiences go it's one of the best.' This little exchange typifies one of the most widely recognized and enduring differences between the genders. Men are typically lustful, novelty-seeking and interested in casual sex, as compared with women, who prefer to incorporate sex within the context of a secure and 'meaningful' relationship. In the classic courtship encounter, a man invests time and money in wining, dining and 'chatting up' a woman to whom he is sexually attracted; she withholds sexual favours while assessing his personality, prospects and sincerity.

Again, it may be necessary to state that the difference is not absolute. Some women are very lustful and adventure-seeking and some men are more interested in relationships than in sex. The difference applies only on average.

The extent of separation and overlap can be assessed empirically in a number of different ways. The British psychologist Hans Eysenck (1976) devised a questionnaire which contained a wide variety of items relating to different aspects of sexual behaviour and attitudes, and administered it to several hundred people. The most striking difference between men and women appeared in connection with 'permissive' issues such as extra-marital sex, mate-swapping, orgies and pornography. Statements such as 'I believe in taking my pleasures where I find them', 'I would vote for a law that permitted polygamy', 'The thought of an illicit relationship excites me' and 'I like to look at sexy pictures' were endorsed about twice as often by men as women, whereas statements like 'Sex is not all that important to me', 'The idea of mate-swapping is extremely distasteful to me' and 'Conditions have to be just right to get me excited sexually' were endorsed about twice as often by women. Thus the men emerged as much more libidinous and adventure-seeking than women overall.

Adding up the scores of men across forty such items produced scores that formed two overlapping bell-shaped graphs very similar to those obtained by graphing the height distributions of men and women (see Figure 1). Thus most men, but not all, are macho as regards their sexual attitudes and preferences, while most women, but not all, are relatively coy and reserved.

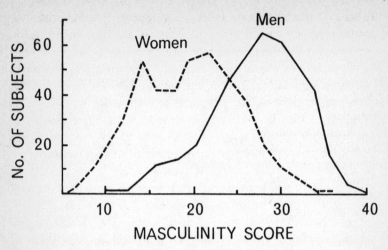

Figure 1   Distribution of scores of men and women on a masculinity-femininity sex attitudes inventory (from Eysenck, 1976).

Sexual fantasies

Next, consider the kinds of things that people report thinking about in their fantasies. This is more relevant to the sexual nature of men and women than comparisons of actual sexual behaviour, because fantasies are less constrained by partner preferences and social expectations. In 1987 I reported a survey in which large numbers of men and women were asked to describe in written, narrative form details of their favourite sexual fantasy. Since they were invited to do this anonymously, there was little likelihood of conscious inhibition of responses.

When a content analysis of these self-reported fantasies was conducted (Table 1) it became clear that the typical fantasies of men and women were quite different. By far the most common element in male fantasies was group sex or sex with two other women; for example, 'being tied to a bed with six or more naked women licking, kissing and fellating me'. Thirty-one per cent of men included elements of group sex in their fantasies; the equivalent figure for women was only 15 per cent (Wilson, 1987a).

Table 1 Main elements of anonymously reported sexual fantasies (in percentages)

Fantasies	Men (N = 291)	Women (N = 409)
Group sex	31	15
Voyeuristic/fetishistic	18	7
Steady partner incorporated	14	21
Identified people (other than partner)	8	8
Setting romantic/exotic	4	15
Rape/force	4	13
Sado-masochism	7	7
None	5	12
Everything	3	0
No answer	21	19

Note: Columns total more than 100 because categories are not mutually exclusive.
Source: Wilson, 1987a.

The second most common theme in the male fantasies could be described as visual or voyeuristic, referring to clothing such as black stockings and suspenders, sexy underwear, leather, or nurses' uniforms; for example, 'A sixteen-year-old virgin dressed in a short-skirted school uniform and who wears a hairband all the time'. Eighteen per cent of men had fetishistic elements like this in their favourite fantasy, but very few women did.

Other primarily male elements, perhaps related to the visual emphasis, were details of anatomy, reference to the age or race of the partner, and descriptions of the sexual activity that was engaged in. Only very occasionally would women refer to anonymous physical characteristics such as the size of the man's penis, the hairiness of his chest or his ethnic origins.

The most common element in female fantasies was inclusion of the husband or current loved partner (21 per cent). Only 14 per cent of males admitted their wives or current partners into their favourite fantasies. The second typically female characteristic was reference to exotic, romantic settings such as islands, beaches, forests, fields, flowers, waterfalls, moonlight, space and heaven (15 per cent); for example, 'My man making love to me on a quiet beach in the moonlight with the waves lapping over us'. The partner was usually present in these settings, and several women mentioned freedom from distraction, often from children or telephone, as an important aspect. Only 4 per cent of male fantasies included romantic settings such as this.

Another common female element was that of rape or force (13 per cent), although very often this meant being raped by the husband, partner or somebody already desired; for instance, being 'raped by somebody I love'. A much smaller proportion of men (4 per cent) said they would like to be raped by women, and a few fantasized being totally submissive to a female partner.

Although some people might think that women are more reticent with respect to their sex lives, there was no gender difference in willingness to answer this question about sex fantasies. It appeared as part of a larger questionnaire with no compulsion to complete all items. Twenty-one per cent of men left the question blank, compared with 19 per cent of women. However, more than twice as many women as men (12 per cent compared with 5 per cent) stated that they had no sexual fantasies; for example, 'I don't need fantasies because I'm perfectly happy with my man and my sex life.' Three per cent of men, but no women, claimed to fantasize about 'everything'.

If sexual fantasies were scored for 'masculinity–femininity' in the manner that Eysenck scored sexual attitudes and preferences, a similar pattern of overlapping curves would be obtained. The fantasies of men and women have some things in common, but there also tend to be clear differences.

Many other differences between men and women in sexual fantasy patterns can be detected. If fantasies are classified into those that are 'active' (taking the initiative in some sexual activity) and those that are 'passive' (having something done to oneself) it becomes clear that men are much more likely to have active fantasies overall (Figure 2); men also report slightly more passive fantasies than women. Nevertheless, the ratio of active to passive fantasies is much higher for men than for women (Wilson and Lang, 1981).

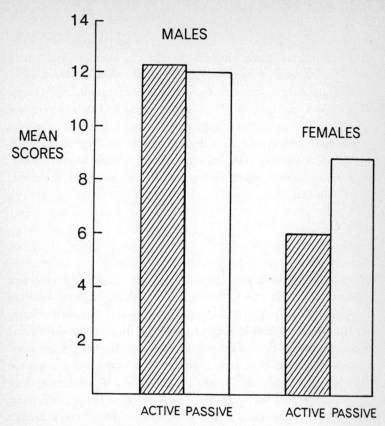

Figure 2 Comparison of men and women on active and passive fantasy scores (from Wilson and Lang, 1981).

There is an interesting difference in the connections between fantasy and reality. Those women who report exploratory fantasies seem to have no difficulty in translating their fantasy into actual behaviour. The correlation between fantasy and activity is very high (Wilson, 1978). The men are not so lucky; those who fantasize about having a lot of different partners are no more successful with women than those men who are less variety-orientated in their fantasies. Supply and demand in the sexual market-place works in such a way that for women an activity is little sooner desired than done, whereas men often have to settle for pornography and masturbation as outlets for their redundant libido.

Another striking difference between the fantasy life of men and women concerned their connections with sexual satisfaction. Generally speaking, those men who reported a great deal of sex fantasy had no partners or were in some sense sexually unfulfilled. Women who engaged in a great deal of fantasy were usually also having an active and satisfying sex life with a loved partner. Thus it seems that men's fantasies often signify sexual frustration, while women's fantasies are awakened or liberated by sexual activity.

Emotional objections

When I first wrote about these differences in male and female sexuality in the *Bulletin of the British Psychological Society* (1979) I was denounced in a letter to the editor written by one of my own female colleagues, who described my paper as 'an apologia for personal rejection'. Her implication was that my argument concerning the relative sexual reticence of women was inspired by a need to rationalize my own inadequacy. While I might be able to defend myself against this charge, the real point is that individual circumstances are irrelevant – the facts concern broad averages that are significant beyond any one person's problems.

Other women wrote to say it couldn't be true because they, personally, felt very sexual. This is again irrelevant from the scientist's point of view. Exceptions can never be used to disprove generalizations; only properly conducted studies which employ large and representative samples of the population can be accepted as worthwhile evidence concerning the distribution of feelings, behavioural preferences and fantasies.

These data concerning the distribution of attitudes and fantasies in the realm of love and sex confirm the stereotype of men as more playful, hedonistic and novelty-seeking and women as more relationship-orientated, serious and mono-gamous in tendency. It would be possible to cite evidence from a variety of other sources such as the content of male and female graffiti, the sales of pornography, the preponderance of female prostitution and of male sex deviation, but this is hardly necessary at this stage. What emerges reliably in all studies of sexual and mating behaviour is a clear separation *between* the distributions for men and women, but with considerable variation *within* each sex that should not be ignored because it gives rise to a definite degree of overlap. The pattern of overlapping distributions illustrated in Figure 1 should be kept firmly in mind because it applies to a lot of attributes both physical and mental that will be discussed in the pages that follow.

I have opened with an outline of sex differences in mating preferences because this area provides some of the most striking differences between men and women. Examples will later be given of sex differences in personality, interests, intellectual and sensory capacities, achievement motivation and various other areas, but similar considerations apply. There are sex differences in many domains that may not be gainsaid by citing individual exceptions to the rule.

Origins of the difference

The question that is perhaps more hotly debated than the existence of the difference between men and women is that concerning the origins of the difference. Here there are two main theories which may be called social learning and evolutionary theory. An outline of these two major theories is given in Figure 3.

Social learning theory

According to the environmentalist or social learning theorists (e.g. Bandura, 1977; Weinreich, 1978) Western society has somehow arrived at a pattern of expectations concerning the desired behaviour of males and females and these 'stereotypes' of

Social learning theory

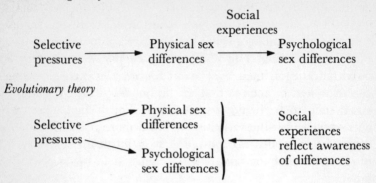

Figure 3 Summary of the two main theories of psychological sex differentiation.

masculinity and femininity are inculcated from the cradle by a programme of rewards and punishments.

Little girls are dressed in pink, told how cute and pretty they are, given dolls to play with, and encouraged to be gentle, passive and dependent. Little boys are dressed in blue, told how brave and ingenious they are, given tractors, construction sets and toy guns to play with, and encouraged to be competitive and aggressive. Later on, girls are taught to be sexually reserved and set their sights on marriage, while boys are taught to chase girls with a view to casual sexual conquests and pursue their careers with entrepreneurial fervour.

The implication is that these stereotypes have been arbitrarily chosen by some abstract decision-making body called 'society' or arrived at by some historical accident and that they could quite readily be dismantled or reversed by appropriate childhood training and media censorship. There is, in fact, plenty of evidence that men and women *are* treated differently by society (Nicholson, 1984), but this does not answer the question of whether social experiences are the cause or effect of sex differences.

In fairness to the social learning theorists I should note that some of them trace the status quo of gender stereotypes to certain basic biological differences. One idea is that the size difference between men and women is the root cause of all sex differences. The argument goes that men, being bigger than women, have imposed their own selfish will and desires upon women, for example, by exercising political and economic power over them and by establishing a 'double standard' of sexual morality in their own favour. Women, they say, have been exploited by men as a result of the genetic accident that caused men to be bigger and stronger. The task of modern, civilized society is therefore to develop a moral code that will compensate for this unfairness, ensuring that brute force does not prevail and giving rise to a more even distribution of power and rewards.

Another biological difference to which some environmentalists trace sex-role differences is the fact that the burden of child-rearing naturally falls upon women rather than men. It is women that get pregnant, have to carry the foetus, and feed the infant in the early stages, whereas men are free to pursue their own interests and pleasures throughout this period. This pattern is carried on through habit even after the children have passed the age of breast-feeding, so that women are assigned continued responsibility for child welfare and education. The result is that women are condemned to domestic bondage, while men seek hedonistic adventures in the wide world.

An anatomical difference between the sexes to which learning theorists sometimes attribute the higher libido and sexual activity of males is the prominence and accessibility of the genitals. Because the boy's penis protrudes, it is much more noticeable to its owner and handy for masturbation than the girl's reproductive organs, which are tucked away from sight and feel and are therefore less of a temptation. The earlier and more frequent masturbation of the boy is then said to be responsible for his greater obsession with sexual pleasure.

When a girl begins to menstruate, she may feel proud to be grown-up at last, but the physical changes she undergoes are not likely to bring her obvious sexual pleasure. A boy, on the other hand, starts to have erotic dreams and frequently finds himself with an unsolicited erection. Like it or not, he can hardly fail to be aware of his genitals or of their potential as a source of pleasure. (Nicholson, 1984, p. 142)

The truth of these assertions is not really questioned by evolutionary theorists. What really identifies these three elaborations as types of social learning theory is the belief that men and women otherwise have much the same feelings, instincts and inclinations. If it were not for these disadvantages deriving from physical circumstances, the social theorists say, women would exhibit the same kind of independent and exploratory personality and aspire to and enjoy the same pursuits as men – competitive careers, casual sex with multiple partners and so on. Extreme social learning theorists presume that the brains, motives, styles of thinking, feelings and innermost desires of women would be indistinguishable from those of men were it not for the handicaps of being small, having a womb, breasts and hidden genitals, and the different social conditioning experienced in the course of their lives.

Evolutionary theory

In complete contrast to social learning theory, the evolutionary viewpoint (Symons, 1979; Wilson, 1981a) is that those selective forces responsible for producing the differing physical stature and reproductive equipment of men and women are capable of producing differences in male and female brains as well. Furthermore, there would be definite advantages in doing so. Such brain differences would manifest themselves in instincts and emotions, fantasies and desires, preferences and motives, leading to behaviour that would serve the interests of the individual and ultimately ensure the survival of his or her genes into the next generation. In this connection it is important to realize that the interests of male and female animals are not always the same. Distinctive strategies of behaviour can be seen to serve the reproductive effectiveness of males and females respectively.

This general viewpoint is sometimes called the 'selfish gene' or socio-biological approach to understanding animal behaviour. The underlying assumption is that our bodies and brains are merely transient machines geared to the preservation and proliferation of our genes. In other words, genes are the units to be considered in the struggle for survival – not the animals themselves or 'the good of the species'. Most modern biologists are coming around to accepting this point of view.

Suppose that male animals have become specialized as hunters and females as child-rearers, what differences would we expect to see? First, we would expect a number of physical differences: males would be faster and stronger and geared particularly to short-term performance. Their muscular bodies would be well equipped for brief bursts of energy, but their metabolism would render them more susceptible to heart disease. Females would be constructed with broader hips for childbirth (though disadvantageous for running) and a built-in food supply for the infant (breasts). A body geared to endurance under conditions of environmental privation (e.g. one storing energy reserves in the form of fat deposits) would be appropriate to females rather than one designed for short-term energy expenditure.

Secondly, we would expect to observe a number of mental and emotional differences supporting this general specialization of function (see Table 2). Males would be more brave and ruthless, so as to be more effective in battle and defence against marauders. They might also develop high-level spatial intelligence that would help them explore the environment, wield weapons and throw projectiles accurately. At the same time, females would be expected to develop the qualities of protectiveness, nurturance and loyalty that would support their mother role, together with a concern with security that would manifest itself as anxiety or fear in threatening environments. In advanced mammals we might also expect the females to develop special communication skills, so that cultural experience could be transmitted effectively to the offspring. Verbal fluency and social intuition would be obvious human examples of such interpersonal skills.

Since individuals who displayed these attributes would

Table 2   Gender differences expected on the basis of evolutionary theory and observed empirically

Males	*Females*
Physical	
Greater size and strength	Lesser size and strength
Capacity for short-term energy output	Capacity for endurance
Mental	
Spatial and mathematical skills	Verbal and social skills
Logic	Empathy
Temperamental	
Dominance	Submission
Rank-related aggression	Defensive aggression
Independence	Attachment/nurturance
Psychopathy	Anxiety
Sensation-seeking	Security-seeking
Sexual initiation and exploration	Sexual selectivity and relationship-seeking

Source: Symons, 1979; Seward and Seward, 1980; Ellis, 1986.

perform their sex role more successfully, their genes would have superior survival value, and so we would expect progressive differentiation of physical and mental equipment as parallel evolutionary developments. If men and women did not show biologically based differences of the kind described, evolutionary theorists would wonder why not. In fact, these very differences are the ones that are observed, fairly universally, regardless of species or culture, time or place.

Reproductive competition

The broad picture of sexual differentiation painted above is actually oversimplified. Another important factor in determining the direction of evolution, and perhaps ultimately the only factor that needs to be considered, is reproductive success. In order to pass on its genes to the next generation an animal has to do more than just survive the environment; he or she has to mate successfully with a member of the opposite sex and raise offspring who themselves will be reproductively successful. Individuals who do not breed are doomed to genetic extinction.

Now in this domain it is clear that the optimal strategies for males and females are quite different. At least this is so for mammals, in which the burden of child production falls on the female. In mammals, the offspring grow inside the body of the female and are dependent on her for succour for some time thereafter. Later on in life the protection of two parents may be better than one, but that is usually much less essential. Generally speaking, mothers invest more in their offspring than do fathers.

For the male, multiple partnerships may be profitable. Theoretically he has the capacity to impregnate several females at the same time, or at least in quick succession, so that their periods of pregnancy overlap. He invests little time and energy in the act of fatherhood and it is therefore to his genetic advantage to distribute his sexual attentions widely. If there is any chance at all that some of the offspring he has sired will survive to sexual maturity themselves, then he maximizes his breeding potential by sequestering several mates or even behaving promiscuously, moving quickly from one female to the next. Impregnating the 'wrong' female at one time (one that is not ideally 'fit', genetically speaking) does not preclude getting the 'right' one pregnant on another occasion. Millions of male sperm are generated for every one egg produced by the female, so wastage is relatively unimportant. Whereas a woman produces only a few hundred eggs in her entire lifetime, a man could theoretically fertilize every woman in Britain with a single ejaculation. This capacity is inevitably associated with the evolution of polygamous urges in men.

Female choice

The female is in a very different position. Once pregnant, she is out of circulation for some time. This includes the entire period of pregnancy and lactation, perhaps even longer if we count the early care of the infant, and this amounts to a very significant proportion of her breeding life. She has little to gain from promiscuous or multiple matings and a great deal to lose, especially when lethal sexually transmitted diseases are epidemic.

By maintaining a degree of reserve and control over her sexual arousability a female can give herself time to select males on certain important criteria. One major basis of choice will be the degree of genetic fitness shown by the male – in terms of health, physical skills, mental ingenuity and other attributes that increase the chances that her offspring sired by him will survive. Another criterion might be the willingness of the male to commit himself to staying around to help care for her during pregnancy and to support the offspring. Elaborate courtship rituals that extend the male's investment in the mating sequence will effectively ensure that he is not committed elsewhere and that he is 'sincere' enough in his affection not to abandon his mate immediately after sexual consummation. The female distaste for 'wham, bam, thank you, ma'am' sex has deep biological significance.

An interesting demonstration of female control over the occurrence of intercourse has been provided by Peplau, Rubin and Hill (1977). Studying a large number of dating couples on American campuses they found that the length of time they would go out together before sexual 'intimacy' first occurred depended on various characteristics of the female partner, such as her religion and previous experience. The characteristics of the men were irrelevant. It thus appears that the willingness of men to have intercourse may be taken for granted; it is women that decide whether and when it will take place.

A similar conclusion can be reached on the strength of studies in Californian singles bars of optimal pick-up lines. For a man, what he says is crucial to whether or not he will be successful in getting off with a potential partner. Success rates vary from zero with openers like 'Let's go back to my place right now' and 'Bet I can drink you under the table' to around 50 per cent with more respectful lines like 'Excuse me, my name is Robert. I've been watching you for some time and can't help finding you extremely attractive. Would you allow me to buy you a drink?' In the case of a woman chatting up a man in this situation, it makes little difference what she says; almost any opening line is 100 per cent successful.

Virginity was once held to be so important that girls were afraid their boyfriend would lose respect for them if they allowed him to 'go all the way'. Since he would be bound to boast of his conquest to all his friends, this would probably also diminish her marriage prospects. Today, pre-marital sex has become so commonplace that a young woman often fears that she will lose her boyfriend if she does not permit intercourse within a reasonable period of time. Christensen and Gregg (1970) found that nearly a quarter of their sample of college women had 'given in' to their first sexual experience without feeling desire on their own part. Rather, they had yielded either to force or some sense of obligation to their boyfriend. Less than 3 per cent of men questioned gave answers that could be classified the same way. Similarly, when Bardwick (1971) asked college women why they had first engaged in intercourse, the answers she obtained were typically along the following lines: 'Well, a great strain not to. Fairly reluctant for a while, but then I realized it had become a great big thing in the relationship and it would disintegrate the relationship. . . . I wanted to also.' 'He'd leave me if I didn't sleep with him.' 'Mostly to see my boyfriend's enjoyment.' 'I gave in to Sidney because I was lonely.'

Very few of the girls interviewed said they had started having sex because they wanted to. Usually it was regarded as a price that had to be paid for continuation of a relationship, or it was an attempt to prove to their boyfriend that they loved him. Despite the great increase in permissiveness in our society over the last few decades, the motives and concerns of the two sexes remain quite different.

The characteristically female trait of coyness makes its appearance very early on in life. At around the age of one or two, little girls are observed to hide their eyes from strangers in a manner that seems to express something half-way between embarrassment and flirtation. This gesture is more typical when the stranger is an adult man other than the father and is seldom observed in little boys. That it is an instinctual behaviour pattern rather than one learned by imitation is suggested by the fact that it also occurs in girls who are born blind and who would therefore have no chance to learn it off other girls or adult women. The seductive element in this gesture has led some ethologists to interpret it as a ritual invitation to chase (Eibl-Eibesfeldt, 1971). They note that a very similar sequence of making eye contact with a man and then modestly diverting the gaze is shown by adult women at parties and other sexually charged situations. This sequence is perceived by men as appropriate and appealing, whereas brazen staring and overly explicit invitations are considered 'unfeminine' and apt to be counterproductive.

There are a great many other deductions that may be made from the 'parental investment theory', as it is often called (Trivers, 1972). For example, we would expect the motives for extra-marital sex to be different for men and women, with men committing adultery primarily for the sake of novelty and women inclining towards adultery when they perceive the other man as superior or more attentive than their husband. Similarly, we would expect jealousy to centre on the act of sexual penetration in the case of men and fear of losing the attention of the mate (the relationship) on the part of women. We would expect women to be less easily aroused by visual stimuli and slower to warm up sexually. We would expect competition between males to be more severe than that between females, with the result that successful high-ranking males would monopolize more than their fair share of females, and the others miss out to some extent. This would lead to a situation in which sexual 'perversions' would be more common in men than women and prostitution would be aimed almost entirely at male clients. Surveys and observational evidence discussed by Symons (1979) and Wilson (1981a) generally support these expectations.

Some of these points will be taken up later. In the meantime, let us look at some evidence which might help us to choose between biological (evolutionary) and social learning theories of the sex differences outlined above. It is, of course, possible to argue that both theories apply, with social learning reinforcing and accentuating the extent of the gender differentiation to which our biology initially inclines us. This compromise position will also be discussed in subsequent chapters.

2 · *Evidence from Human Biology*

If there are differences between males and females with respect to mating instincts, temperament and intellectual functioning, these are bound to be mediated by the effects of hormones on the brain, just as the hormones determine anatomical differences between the sexes. Although it is widely believed that sexual differentiation depends on the sex chromosomes (XX or XY), these chromosomes can only affect the body and behaviour via the action of circulating hormones.

The sex hormones are a group of closely related stereo-chemicals, each having an individual shape that allows them to fit like door keys into their receptor sites which are located mainly in the lower part of the brain. These receptors can only be operated by their own particular hormone or a close chemical substitute. If that hormone is not available in the bloodstream, or if the site has been blocked by some impostor which fits the keyhole but does not turn the lock, that part of the brain will not be activated. The effect of hormones, therefore, depends both upon their concentration in the blood and the sensitivity of the receptors, the latter being mainly a question of the microanatomy of the brain (Silver and Feder, 1964).

Major sex hormones

The most important sex hormones are oestrogens, which cause the female to be receptive and physically desirable to the male;

26

progesterones, which prepare for and support pregnancy in the female; and androgens – particularly testosterone – which make us sexually assertive and predatory. Androgens are naturally more prevalent in males (being produced in large quantities by the testes), but the small amount that is present in females (produced mainly by the adrenal cortex) seems to be largely responsible for such sexual assertiveness as women show. Apart from the effects on sexual behaviour and reproductive function noted above, the sex hormones also determine bodily structures such as the genitals, secondary sex characteristics such as hair distribution and depth of voice, and sex-typical behaviours such as male competitiveness and female nurturance.

Much of the evidence concerning the functions of these hormones comes from studies of the effects of administering to people of one gender hormones that are naturally produced in greater quantities by the other (cross-hormone intervention). If women are given injections of the 'male' hormone testosterone, they tend to show increased libido and aggressiveness (typically male traits): thus testosterone has sometimes been used to treat women who complain of insufficient sexual responsiveness (Carney, Bancroft and Mathews, 1978). The danger is that, if too much is given, the woman may begin to develop masculine physical characteristics like a deep voice, hair on the chin and an enlarged clitoris.

If oestrogens are given to men, the reverse happens; their normally high level of libido and aggressiveness is reduced. For this reason oestrogen has been used to treat violent criminals and intransigent sex offenders. The problem here is that the man may grow breasts and become fat about the hips, and so other forms of 'chemical castration', such as cyproterone acetate, are increasingly preferred by forensic psychiatrists (Bancroft, 1975). Of course there are serious ethical objections to the chemical treatment of prisoners, but these are beyond the scope of this discussion.

The fact that hormones are capable of shifting people's behaviour in directions traditionally recognized as masculine or feminine, without the individual concerned knowing which chemicals – if any – they have been given, is powerful evidence for a biological theory of psychological sex differences. It is difficult to imagine how this effect could be accounted for in terms of social-role learning. Similarly, the unmistakable fluctuations in temperament and libido that occur in connection with a woman's cycle, which are known to be related to cyclic changes in her hormone secretions, cannot be accounted for by learning theory. For example, women appear to be sexually receptive at the mid-cycle (high oestrogen) phase, and sexually aggressive around the time of their period, when oestrogen is at its lowest level (Udry and Morris, 1968; Bancroft, 1988).

Pre-natal hormone effects

Sex hormones begin to influence our personality and sexuality well before birth. All foetuses begin development along a female course, but the male has testes which produce testosterone, and this hormone is the one that most strikingly alters the development of all the baby's bodily structures, including the brain.

Particularly impressive evidence for this effect has been provided by June Reinisch of Rutgers University, New Jersey. She investigated the personality development of boys and girls whose mothers had been treated with steroid hormones during pregnancy (a procedure which used to be followed to maintain a pregnancy thought to be at risk). Children whose mothers had been given progestines (synthetic progesterones that simulate the action of male androgens in many ways) were found to be more independent, individualistic, self-assured and self-sufficient than those whose mothers had been treated with oestrogens (female hormones). When children born under these unusual chemical circumstances of the womb were compared with 'untreated' siblings, the same personality differences were observed (Reinisch, 1977).

Indications are that the middle third of pregnancy is critical with respect to sex differentiation in the brain, at least in humans (Ellis and Ames, 1987). In lower mammals such as rats sexual differentiation of the brain may continue until after birth.

The significance of pelvic shape

Another fascinating demonstration of biological influences on social and sexual behaviour is seen in the work of a German physician, Dr W.S. Schlegel (1975). His starting-point was the fact that males tend to have a funnel-shaped pelvis which is narrow at the bottom, while females tend to have a tube-shaped pelvis which is relatively broad at the bottom. The size of the pelvic outlet is of obvious importance in childbirth, and thus natural selection would account for this difference. The male pelvis is designed for running; the female pelvis is a compromise between one that is good for running and one that is good for producing babies. However, pelvic shape differs from person to person. There are some men with tube-shaped pelvises and some women with funnel-shaped pelvises. In fact, when the pelvic widths of large numbers of men and women are graphically plotted, the distributions overlap rather in the same way as do height and sexual attitudes (although not quite to the same extent).

Assuming that pelvic shape is determined by pre-natal androgen secretion (which seems beyond doubt), and if later sexual and social behaviour is also determined by pre-natal androgen secretion (as our biological theory supposes), then we might expect to find correlations within each sex between sex-role behaviour and pelvic shape. This is precisely what Schlegel found. Men and women with male-type pelvises tended to behave in a stereotypically masculine manner, while men and women with female-type pelvises tended to behave in a feminine manner. The male-type pelvis went with leadership and dominance of personality, active sexuality and a preference for younger sex partners in men and women alike. The female-type pelvis was associated with empathy, suggestibility and compliance, as well as a preference for older sex partners. In other words, masculine and feminine behaviour seems to be determined by the same hormonal factors that originally produced the skeletal features of the pelvis, namely the amount of androgen secretion occurring during foetal development.

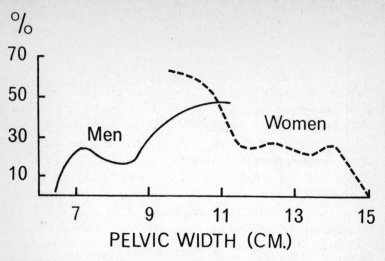

Figure 4 Relative frequency of divorce for men and women having certain types of pelvic structure (from Schlegel, 1975).

Schlegel also found that homosexual men tended to have female-type pelvises, which is not unexpected considering that hormonal factors have been implicated in male homosexuality (Dorner, 1976; Gladue, Green and Hellman, 1984; Ellis and Ames, 1987). Furthermore, men and women with pelvises atypical of their gender were much more likely to have suffered broken marriages (Figure 4). If maintaining a stable marriage can be taken as an indication of satisfactory sex-role performance then this finding is also consistent with the idea that masculinity and femininity are biologically determined.

Schlegel's finding has since been partially replicated by Wilson and Reading (1989). In a sample of seventy women attending a London pre-natal clinic it was found that those who were feminine in personality and traditional in their sex-role attitudes were both wider in pelvic outlet and more sexually satisfied than masculine feminist women (Figure 5).

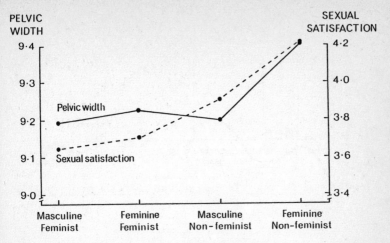

Figure 5 Mean pelvic width and sexual satisfaction scores for four groups of women classified on the basis of masculinity–femininity and traditionalism–feminism questionnaires (from Wilson and Reading, 1989).

Depth of voice

Such research supports the idea that sex hormones operate simultaneously on physical structures and psychological pre-dispositions such as personality and emotions. Other studies along these lines concern the correlates of depth of voice, which is another obvious way in which men typically differ from women.

Male voices are deepened under the influence of sex hormones at puberty. But some are deepened more than others (basses as opposed to tenors) and some women's voices are also deepened to some degree (contraltos compared with sopranos). Some German research (Meuser and Nieschlag, 1977) has shown that deep-voiced male choristers (basses and baritones) have a higher ratio of male to female hormones than tenors, and Wilson (1984) found parallel differences in the personalities of opera singers of different voice categories. Lower-voiced singers were not only taller than higher-voiced members of their own sex, but they were also less emotional ('hysterical') in personality,

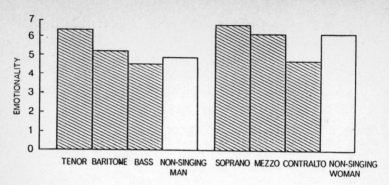

Figure 6 Mean ratings of the emotionality of six groups of opera singers and non-singing controls by their close associates (from Wilson, 1984).

and higher in libido as determined by items such as the number of backstage affairs that they admitted to. Mean ratings on the personality dimension of 'emotionality' for singers of six voice categories, as well as non-singing controls, are shown in Figure 6. Within each sex the higher-voiced singers are perceived by their colleagues as more emotional.

Such findings further confirm the fact that sex hormones have power to affect psychological characteristics, including traditional sex role behaviour, as well as anatomical structures that differentiate men and women.

Genetic variations in sexuality

Experiments with animals show that individual differences in libido are fixed for life. If male rats are classified with respect to their characteristic frequency of copulation and then castrated, the sexual activity of both high and low libido groups is reduced to near zero. Then, if they are given replacement injections of testosterone in massive doses, restoring to them a great deal more male hormone than would occur naturally, the individual rats are returned only to their own initial level of sexual activity. Those that were highly active sexually before castration are reactivated to the same high level, while those that were fairly uninterested before castration revert to their same low frequency of copulation (Bermant and Davidson, 1974). Apparently, male sex drive is to a large extent set by brain mechanisms which only require a certain threshold level of testosterone for full operation. This would explain why the sex drive of normal men is not further enhanced by testosterone injections. In all probability they are already at threshold in this respect. However, the sex drive of women, or men who are deficient in testosterone for some reason (e.g. older men or men who have suffered accidental castration), is increased by additional testosterone (Bancroft, 1988).

The research of Hans Eysenck and colleagues at the London Institute of Psychiatry (Eysenck, 1976) has shown that variations in human libido, within each sex, are also strongly influenced by heredity. Eysenck found that the differences within male and female groups were at least as striking as average differences between the sexes (recall the pattern illustrated in Figure 1), and these within-gender variations were subjected to classical heritability analysis using large samples of identical and fraternal twins. This is a procedure that enables us to find out how much of the variation on a characteristic is due to heredity and how much to the environment.

Identical twins are genetically identical, being the outcome of the splitting of a single egg fertilized by a single sperm. By contrast, fraternal twins on average share only 50 per cent of their genes, being the outcome of two eggs fertilized at around the same time by two sperm. Thus any trait which is largely determined by genetic factors is manifested in a similiar fashion by identical twins, while fraternal twins are much less alike, and these facts can be used to estimate the amount of heritability of a given trait. By such logic Eysenck was able to determine that a substantial part of the variability with respect to libido and masculinity–femininity of attitudes within each sex is due to genetic causes (around 45 per cent for women and 60 per cent for men). This being the case, it is most unlikely that differences between men and women could be accounted for entirely by sex-role learning experiences.

It may be tempting for the reader to imagine that because

heritability analysis finds that only around half of the variation in libido and maculinity–femininity of personality is contributed by the genes, then the rest must be determined by social role learning. However, such a conclusion would not be warranted. The discovery that an attribute is influenced by the environment tells us nothing about *which factors* in the environment are important. Physical disturbances are very likely more significant than social experiences.

We already know that the chemical environment of the foetus before birth, including variations due to maternal diet, drugs and stress, can have profound effects on sexual development (Ellis and Ames, 1987), and this has nothing to do with social roles or learning. Other significant environmental factors might include birth injury (such as that due to anoxia or forceps delivery), infantile meningitis and encephalitis, or even falling off a tricycle and bumping one's head at the age of four. It is known that brain injuries of this kind can give rise to anomalies of sexuality such as transvestitism and loss of libido (Flor-Henry, 1987). All of these are environmental effects, but they are physical effects on the brain and not connected with what we normally think of as upbringing or social influences. Thus evidence in support of social learning theory cannot be obtained 'by default' from genetic analysis.

The studies described above are merely illustrative of a vast amount of evidence concerning the biological foundations of gender differences and sexual behaviour. One could also cite the studies of John Money and his colleagues on the adrenogenital syndrome (Money, 1973). This is a genetic defect which may cause the adrenal gland in a girl to secrete too much androgen. Although such individuals are treated by society as girls from birth, they grow up to display tomboy characteristics, such as a preference for male clothes, hair-styles, toys and games, assertiveness, ambitiousness and a lack of interest in marriage and the maternal role. The significance of anomalies such as this is discussed in greater detail in Chapter 5.

Brain differences

In recent years it has become possible to locate the precise brain regions responsible for male and female behaviour. There is no single brain switch that decides whether we are male or female, but probably separate levers controlling degrees of maleness and femaleness in different aspects of sex-role behaviour. For example, sexual orientation (whether we prefer male or female partners) overlaps with, but is not identical with, other sex-typical attitudes and behaviours.

The important brain areas so far discovered are all located in or around an area of the midbrain called the hypothalamus, which is conveniently located just above the pituitary gland, which controls the entire glandular system. The preoptic anterior nucleus seems to regulate masculine brain functions like mounting in response to female signals – in humans this area of the hypothalamus is about twice as large in males as females. Transplants of tissue from this area from male to female brains (so far done only in rats) cause recipient females to behave in male ways.

Two areas seem particularly involved in female sexual behaviour, the ventromedical nucleus, which controls a cyclic release of hormones (in contrast to the tonic male pattern), and the anterior nucleus, which controls receptiveness to mounting. These areas can also be seen under a microscope to differ between male and female brains, the connections being much more dense and complex in female brains.

Apart from the hypothalamic nuclei determining sexual behaviour itself, there are very likely some broader types of brain difference betwen men and women. For example, studies of brain lateralization suggest that male brains are differentiated from female brains with respect to the degree of specialization of the right hemisphere (McGlone, 1980). In men the right hemisphere of the brain is highly developed for spatial functioning of the kind required by astronomy, map-reading and tennis-playing, whereas in women it is more like a back-up to the left (verbal–sequential) side of the brain. Thus the effect of damage to the male brain depends very much on the *site* of the lesion; in female brains it is the *extent* of damage that is critical. The question of male–female differences in mental ability is discussed further in Chapter 6.

It is impossible within the scope of this book to give a complete review of evidence relating to male–female brain differences. Hopefully, the examples given will provide some insight into the manner in which they may be, and have been, investigated. Few scientists who have properly examined the relevant evidence are disposed to doubt the important role played by pre-natal hormones in laying the foundations for personality, cognitive functioning and social and sexual behaviour in adulthood. In particular, the sex hormones, acting via the brain, determine to a very great extent the male–female differences that we think of as 'traditional' or 'stereotypical'.

The inertia of environmentalism

Unfortunately many of these facts about the role of hormones and the brain in determining behavioural sex differences were discovered only in the last few decades, by which time American psychologists and sociologists were heavily committed to an environmentalist, social learning position. A few of them have had the open-mindedness and courage to recant on their earlier position, as did John Money and his colleagues to a considerable extent by the late 1960s (Money and Ehrhardt, 1972) and J.R. Udry in the third edition of his widely used textbook on marriage:

The first edition of this text, based on information available in 1965, presented a thoroughly sociological explanation of the origin of sex differences in behaviour. At that time I argued that sex differences were probably completely determined by socialization, and that any innate predisposition to different behaviour by the two sexes was trivial. The information available today invalidates my previous explanations. Evidence on the role of sex hormones in differentiating the behaviour of other animals has been accumulating for two decades. . . . Now the human data makes it possible for us to begin sorting out sex differences into those underwritten by biology, however culturally embellished, and those that are genuine cultural options. . . . It is no longer tenable to believe that males and females are born into the world with the same behavioural predisposition. (Udry, 1974, p. 45)

Among the differences that Udry considers to be definitely connected with the presence or absence of foetal androgens are the male tendencies towards dominance, competition and high energy expenditure and the female predisposition to care for infants. He goes on to note:

If we are thorough-going in our determination to eliminate sex role differences, we must recognize that it will be necessary to work at cross-purposes with the natural propensity of the organism. Specifically, we will have to reward dominance and punish submissiveness in women, while we reward submissiveness and punish dominance in men. No one can be sure what other problems such socialization might create. (Ibid., p. 49)

Another admission of conversion on the basis of scientific evidence came from Diane Halpern who wrote a book on *Sex Differences in Cognitive Abilities* after years of teaching the socialization theory to 'Psychology of Women' classes in California.

At the time it seemed to me clear that between-sex differences in thinking abilities were due to socialization practices, artifacts and mistakes in the research, and bias and prejudice. After reviewing a pile of journal articles that stood several feet high and numerous books and book chapters that dwarfed the stack of journal articles, I changed my mind. . . . The data collected within the last few years provide a convincing case for the importance of biological variables. (Halpern, 1986, p. vii)

It is brave of Udry and Halpern to admit that new evidence compelled them to change their minds about the origin of sex roles. More commonly, the environmentalists have become further entrenched in their attempts to justify their previous position.

Some American psychologists seem so steeped in the environmentalist orientation of historical giants such as Watson, Thorndike and Skinner that they actually *equate* the words 'psychological' and 'environmental'. This is apparent, for example, in the introduction to Maccoby and Jacklin's very influential book *The Psychology of Sex Differences*. They say: '*Psychological* processes are stressed, but this is not to deny the impact of biology. An individual's sex is obviously both a biological and a social fact. . . . Few psychologists now believe that all newborn human individuals are alike in their potential reactions to the experiences they will have' (Maccoby and Jacklin, 1974).

Despite this concession to the newly recognized importance of biological factors, Maccoby and Jacklin seek to evade responsibility for dealing with them, claiming them to be outside the expertise of psychologists: 'The writers are neither geneticists nor biologists, and are therefore not equipped to undertake an in depth account of these factors' (p. 3). Maccoby and Jacklin do discuss certain genetic and hormonal effects upon aggression, dominance and intellectual functioning in the course of their book, but one is left with the impression that they regard social factors as somehow more 'psychological' than biological determinants of behaviour.

This is somewhat alien to the British view of psychology as the science of behaviour, without prejudice as to its major causes and, in fact, as the area of overlap between biological and sociological disciplines (Eysenck and Wilson, 1976). This is no doubt one of the reasons why evolutionary theories of behaviour have always been better received in Britain than in the United States. The American political ethos has always been guided by the 'office boy to President' fantasy, hence US psychologists have been loath to entertain theories which appear to set genetic limits on behaviour or achievement. It is significant that many

American researchers who do recognize the importance of evolutionary biology to the understanding of individual differences have been reclassified as 'socio-biologists', as though this is a separate discipline, not part of psychology.

While referring to Maccoby and Jacklin's book, we might note that a preference for environmentalist studies of sex differences could also have been dictated by their self-confessed feminist bias: 'We are both feminists (of different vintages, and one perhaps more militant than the other!), and although we have tried to be objective about the value-laden topics discussed in this book, we know that we cannot have succeeded entirely' p. 3). In fact, Maccoby and Jacklin succeed better than most in producing a book worthy of scientific consideration, but is is unfortunate that so many books on the topic of sex differences are written by dedicated feminists whose political aims take precedence over objective facts in the matter. They write books to accompany courses called 'Women's Studies' rather than 'Individual Differences', and their concern is not so much with what *is*, but what they think *ought to be* (Levin, 1988).

Genetic feminism

Since the above may give the impression that feminism is always identified with radical environmentalism, I should note in passing that this is not necessarily the case. There are many brands of feminism available to the unwary consumer, some of which do concede the pre-eminence of biological factors in sex-role differentiation. The fact that the prototypic human form is female rather than male before the pre-natal hormones take effect has led some feminists to propose that women are therefore the more 'natural' and superior sex. A few have gone even further and argued that masculinity is a kind of biological aberration, like Down's syndrome, which might be eliminated by genetic engineering:

It is now technically possible to reproduce without the aid of males and to produce only females. We must begin immediately to do so. The male is a biological accident. The 'Y' (male) gene is an incomplete set of chromosomes. In other words, the male is an incomplete female, a walking abortion, aborted at the gene state. . . . Many women will for a while continue to think they dig men, but as they become accustomed to female society and as they become absorbed in their projects, they will eventually come to see the utter uselessness and banality of the male. (Solanis, 1970)

This particular statement comes from the lunatic fringe of feminism and is probably not endorsed by the majority of women who call themselves feminists. It does, however, illustrate the blending of pseudoscience and politics (and in this case explicit man-hating) that characterizes much of feminist writing.

The truth is that boys and girls are born anatomically different and with different psychological inclinations (on average). Neither sex is biologically more 'natural' than the other; nature has dictated that the two sexes will occur in roughly equal numbers. Nor is one sex superior to the other overall. Superiority in this sense is an *evaluative* rather than *scientific* concept. Each sex excels in particular tasks and is endowed with certain qualities which in terms of species survival and human progress are probably about equally important.

3 · Evidence from Animals and Other Cultures

The biological evidence presented in the previous chapter is perhaps the most convincing support for the evolutionary theory of sex differences. Nevertheless, we may further confirm it by looking at comparisons across different species of animal and across different human cultures. This is particularly pertinent to the frequently voiced assertion that the sex differences we are discussing are peculiar to the stereotypes or upbringing that are provided by 'our society'. Such an argument seems to imply that the sex-role arrangements are very different in other times, places and animal groups. As we shall see, this is not really so; sex differences in other species are sometimes differently organized from our own, but not usually the species that are closest to ourselves. As for the cultural differences that anthropologists frequently refer to with respect to gender roles, these are usually superficial or exaggerated.

The Coolidge Effect

The males of most mammalian species have a definite urge towards seeking variety in their sexual partners. In the laboratory this has been called the 'Coolidge Effect' (Bermant, 1976). If a male rat is introduced to a female rat in a cage, a remarkably high copulation rate will be observed at first. Then, progressively, the male will tire of that particular female and, even though there is no apparent change in her receptivity, he

41

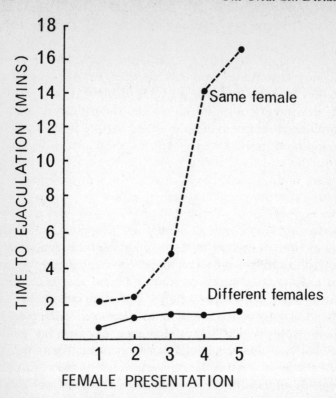

Figure 7 A demonstration of the Coolidge Effect in sheep (from Beamer, Bermant and Clegg, 1960).

eventually reaches a point where he has little apparent libido. However, if the original female is then removed and a fresh one supplied, the male is immediately restored to his former vigour and enthusiam.

The same effect is seen even more strikingly in farm animals such as sheep and cattle (see Figure 7). Rams and bulls are unmistakably resistant to repeating sex with the same female (Beamer, Bermant and Clegg, 1969). Thus for breeding purposes it is unnecessary for a farmer to have more than one male to service all his sheep and cows. A single bull can be relied upon to do the rounds of all the available cows, and a single ram will eventually service all the sheep in his domain.

Donald Symons (1979) of the University of California, Santa Barbara, has pointed out that the term 'indiscriminate' has been applied inaccurately to male sexuality. Male animals do not choose their mates randomly; they identify and reject those that they have already had sex with. In the case of rams and bulls it is notoriously difficult to fool them that a female is unfamiliar. Attempts to disguise an old partner by covering her face and body or masking her vaginal odours with other smells are usually unsuccessful. Somehow she is identified as 'already serviced' and the male moves on to less familiar females. W.S. Gilbert's assertion that 'love unchanged will cloy' (*Trial by Jury*) seems to apply with a vengeance down on the farm.

Bermant (1976) has given an amusing, if somewhat apocryphal, account of the origin of the term 'Coolidge Effect'. The story goes that President and Mrs Coolidge were visiting a government farm in Kentucky one day and after arrival were taken off on separate tours. When Mrs Coolidge passed the chicken pens she paused to ask her guide how often the rooster could be expected to perform his duty. 'Dozens of times a day' was her guide's reply. She was most impressed by this and said, 'Please tell that to the President.' When the President was duly informed of the rooster's performance he was initially dumbfounded. Then a thought occurred to him. 'Was this with the same hen each time?' he inquired. 'Oh no, Mr President, a different one each time' was his host's reply. The President nodded slowly, smiled and said, 'Tell that to Mrs Coolidge!'

Although the Coolidge Effect is somewhat diminished in force within primates, and perhaps especially so in humans who have moral compunctions to deal with in addition, vestiges of it are nevertheless apparent. Before marriage it is usual for men to initiate intercourse at a fairly high frequency with their fiancée. After a few years of marriage, however, the husband's sexual appetite begins to wane and an apparent reversal of libido may even occur, with the now frustrated wife demanding more love-making than her 'tired' husband is able to supply. He, of course, is still perfectly capable of being aroused by his mistresses and office girls and, if fortunate enough to secure an invitation to an orgy, would have little difficulty completing intercourse with two or three anonymous young women in the course of the evening's festivities. Sex therapists see many men who are reported as 'impotent' by their wives but who privately confess to considerable prowess with a succession of mistresses. Clearly, this is more of a social problem than a medical condition.

Data illustrating the Coolidge Effect in human beings have been reported by Wilson (1981a). Large samples of men and women were asked if they were 'getting enough sex at the moment', 56 per cent of men and 41 per cent of women replying that they were not. When asked what their ideal would be, 63 per cent of women said 'more sex with their spouse or steady partner' (compared with 38 per cent of men) and 37 per cent of men said 'more partners' (compared with 18 per cent of women). Separation of the data into results for people of two different generations (younger and older than thirty) showed no change in this sex difference as a result of the new climate of sexual equality in which the younger generation has been raised (Table 3). Evidently partner variety is of greater interest to men than to women, and this difference is reliable and enduring.

Male breeding competition

The inter-male struggle for access to females has been documented in many species. An extreme case is the North American grouse, in which only about one in ten of the males ever gets to mate. Studies of free-ranging Rhesus monkeys show that the top 20 per cent of males in the dominance hierarchy account for about 80 per cent of the copulations and at least half hardly ever achieve copulation, apparently because of social inhibition.

A very similar degree of unevenness in male copulatory success is observed in polygamous tribes such as the Yanamamo in the Amazon (Freedman, 1979). Western society, although superficially monogamous, may well have a comparable infrastructure with a certain proportion of men 'dropping out' altogether from reproductive competition ('wimps', deviants, schizophrenics, alcoholics and tramps), while successful business-

Table 3   Male and female conceptions of the ideal sex life (in percentages)

Age	Male (N = 1,862)		Female (N = 2,905)	
	<30	>30	<30	>30
Not getting enough sex at the moment	55	56	41	41
If not enough, then ideal would be:				
(a) more sex with spouse or steady partner	37	38	62	63
(b) more exciting variations with partner	34	38	24	26
(c) more partners	38	37	20	18

Source: Wilson, 1981b.

men, politicians, actors, television preachers and so on enjoy the favours of several wives, mistresses, groupies, etc.

By contrast, the females of most species including humans (at least in the absence of contraception) achieve their optimal breeding capacity. As Symons (1979) points out, even the most unattractive woman in a village, whom no man would admit to touching, somehow manages to get pregnant every so often.

From the 'group selection' point of view, this could be seen as strengthening the species by increasing the extent to which the superior males – those that are physically healthy, skilful and intelligent – pass on their genes to the next generation in greater proportion. Indeed the pattern of polygyny (one high-ranking male mating with several females) may well be essential to the survival of a species. Groups that did not adopt such a policy would suffer some degree of genetic stagnation and might soon be disadvantaged in relation to those that did.

In any case, the genetic benefits to the individual male who sequesters and impregnates more than his share of females should be sufficient to ensure that male instincts promoting the pursuit of multiple mates would be selected for. Polygyny is therefore the most widespread mating system in the mammalian, primate and human world.

Alternative mating systems

Despite the prevalence of polygyny in the animal world, evolution permits alternative solutions to the problem of optimal mating strategies (Mitchell, 1981). Among our nearest relatives, gorillas adopt the harem system most conspicuously. A dominant male lives with several females and tolerates only one or two young males in his troop who are usually his own sons. In order to maintain the harem he may have to defend it against vigorous attacks from bachelor would-be usurpers. Because size and strength are vital in this form of male competition, they have evolved to be very large, especially in relation to the females of the species. Male gorillas are about twice the size of females, and this size is necessary as a deterrent to rival males who might seek to steal their females. Their genitals, however, are quite small by comparison with other apes – since their females are 'captive', they do not have to impress them or impregnate them on first copulation.

At the other extreme is the gibbon, which displays a kind of monogamous pair-bonding system much like that recommended by moralists for human society and which is otherwise usually seen only in birds. Because the males do not have to fight with each other to obtain or retain mating privileges, there is no significant size difference between the males and females. The gibbon, therefore, can survive as a species without the males being thrown into bloody competition with each other. Purely by instinct, it seems, and without reinforcement by social institutions such as the Church and the law, relatives or public commitment, the gibbons have arrived at a civilized system of monogamy that would delight the puritans. This clearly works for the gibbon, because they have not become extinct.

The question arises as to which of these primates provides the better model for helping us to understand the natural inclinations of the human ape. Genetically we are much closer to the gorilla than to the gibbon, but the size difference between human males and females is not as great as that of the gorilla. Human males are bigger than females by a factor of about 15 per cent of body weight. This is about the same as the sex differential in the size of chimpanzees, who are even more closely related to us genetically (Harcourt and Stewart, 1977). Judging from the body–weight ratio, we would expect both humans and chimps to display a mating pattern that is part-way between those of gorillas and gibbons – some mixture of polygyny and monogamy.

This indeed appears to be the case. Chimps form exclusive consortships that last for a week or two, and privacy is sought for these episodes. But they do not pair-bond for life; the 'honeymoons' are interspersed with examples of harem-building and outright promiscuity. Furthermore, the willingness of the female to accept sexual advances from a particular male depends upon his position in the hierarchy, the vigour of his courtship display, and sometimes even upon the provision of food.

The sexual behaviour of chimpanzees is probably the nearest to our own, which is not surprising given our close genetic relatedness. We appear to have tendencies towards promiscuity and harem-building, as well as towards more or less temporary exclusive attachments, and the relative success of various males depends a great deal on their social status, skill, accomplishment, keenness and willingness to provide.

The gibbon is often held up as an example by people who prefer to think of humans as naturally monogamous creatures. If one primate is naturally monogamous, they say, then humans may also be and, indeed, this certainly shows there is some flexibility in the range of possibilities. But it should be stressed that the gibbon is a very rare species among mammals in this respect. The vast majority of mammals (including higher primates) exhibit some tendency towards polygyny that is apparently related to high levels of competitiveness, aggression and sexual novelty-seeking on the part of the males. Furthermore, the apes that are closest to us in the evolutionary tree tend towards polygyny. The majority of species that practise monogamous pair-bondings are birds, which of course are far removed from humans in evolutionary terms and whose breeding circumstances are very different from our own.

We should ask ourselves whether the behaviour of the third great ape, the orang-utan, has anything to tell us about our natural mating tendencies. Orang-utans may be characterized as the rapists of the jungle. Much of the time they move around as solitary individuals, but, if a male encounters a female, sex is likely to occur. The females sometimes engage in consortships with a favoured male, but at other times they appear to be taken involuntarily and by force. When first assaulted the female orang-utan struggles and cries in distress, but once pinned down and penetrated she seems resigned to her fate (Nadler, 1977). The possibility that human rape is a 'natural' variation of sexual behaviour is discussed in Chapter 7.

A defence that environmentalists sometimes muster against animal analogies is that they are irrelevant, because humans are not animals but, rather, something God-like, or at least far superior to the common brutes. While it is true that our use of tools and language has raised us far above other species as regards cultural development, and no doubt confers more control of our moral destiny, most of our instinctual and emotional reactions date from a much earlier phase of evolutionary development. Some may be traced to the emergence of bipedal man on the African savannahs; others seem to be derivative of our early mammalian heritage, or even our reptilian ancestry (Maclean, 1975).

Man may be a highly advanced and culturally elaborated animal, but he is still an animal, with primitive passions that motivate much of his behaviour, however unwilling we may be to recognize and admit it. To say that this *should* not be so, as the moralists do, is not relevant to the argument that it happens to *be* so. The fact is that humans have a great many needs and desires in common with other species, and the tendency towards male promiscuity and harem-building appears to be in this category. The extent to which brutish instincts can be controlled in favour of higher ideals such as peace and justice is a separate matter, to which we shall return.

It is clear from the observation of various animal species that sex differences in mating strategies are not unique to humans. They occur just as decisively in a wide variety of mammals and primates and they are quite obviously parallel to those seen in human society. Only, in the case of non-human animals, the sex-role learning hypothesis appears much less convincing. Most of these animals arrive at their mating strategies without any obvious social training (although, as Desmond Morris (1979) points out, certain 'perversions' occur if they are cage-reared in isolation from other members of their species and are thus unable to imprint upon an appropriate sex target). If social learning is unnecessary to account for the sex-role behaviour of other animals, why should we suddenly invoke it to explain much the same sexual differentiation in humans? Social factors may be powerful in humans but their effect is only to magnify or suppress sex-role differences, not create them.

The loss of oestrus

Critics of the animal model of human sexuality sometimes also claim that we are not comparable to other animals because the human female has no clearly defined period of sexual receptivity or 'heat'. Women are more or less available for sexual activity at all times of the month, even during menstruation; or, rather, their reservations seem to be much less dependent on simple matters of cyclic physiology. According to some environmentalists, this liberation from cyclic control in the human female takes human sexuality right out of the realm of animal behaviour and allows it to be used in connection with 'higher' sentiments such as love and loyalty. Some ethologists come close to this idea when they say that the loss of oestrus in the human female evolved for the purpose of facilitating pair-bonds between particular males and females, thus leading to stable families and more civilized social living. Morris (1971), for example, has argued that regular, month-round, sexual intercourse between a couple consolidates their love for each other and helps them stay together for the sake of their offspring.

There are several things to say about this. First, the loss of heat in human females does not make our species different in kind; it is merely an extension of a trend that is apparent in the evolutionary line. Most quadruped mammals, such as deer, work on an annual breeding cycle, with one 'rutting' period per year. Primates more usually show a shorter (e.g. monthly) cycle and, generally speaking, those that are closest to humans show the longest period of receptivity within that cycle. Receptivity in the gorilla lasts about two days; in the chimpanzee it lasts about ten days. The human female could be said to have extended oestrus even further than the chimpanzee, but, perhaps more importantly, she has disguised the point of ovulation. She no longer signals her fertility and lack of fertility but is attractive to males pretty well all of the time.

What might be the selective advantage of this change in physiological 'strategy'? Morris's idea of pair-bond consolidation is one possible explanation, but is open to criticism. The main problem is that there is no real evidence that repeated sexual intercourse promotes love. Men eventually tire of sex with the same partner, and passionate love may actually be enhanced by delay of sexual gratification or geographical separation (Wilson and Nias, 1976). Courtly love flourished in the medieval days of chivalry, even in the total absence of sexual consummation.

A better theory of heat loss in the human female has been offered by Donald Symons in his stimulating book, *The Evolution of Human Sexuality* (1979). Male chimpanzees have been observed in the wild to share their catch with females, and particularly females who are in heat (presumably in order to curry sexual favour). Since receiving gifts of meat from hunter males would enhance the survival of the female, it would be to her genetic advantage to conceal times of infertility and be sexually receptive for longer periods of time. Thus Symons suggests that the advantage of gaining continuous male help has led to the continuous sexuality that we observe in the human female. At the same time, the absence of any period of heat, in which control of sexual favours is pretty much lost, would support the selectivity strategy that is important to female reproductive success.

Such a view is, of course, infuriating to the feminist because it implies that what is most unique about human sexual functioning (the extension of female receptiveness or, as some prefer, 'unreceptiveness') has evolved in support of a gender differentiation of labour, with men becoming the providers and women assuming various forms of prostitution. However, we should not reject a scientific theory simply because it is politically discomforting, and Symons's theory of heat loss in the human female may well prove to be the most satisfactory one.

Cross-cultural comparisons

Historical and anthropological comparisons show that the same sex differences within the domain of love and marriage have prevailed in virtually every time and place. Among the ancient Greeks, for example, the male need for sexual variety was openly conceded and a 'double standard' was firmly maintained (Bardis, 1979). It was usual for a husband to have sex with prostitutes, foreign women and slaves, and possibly even teenage boys, while the wife was expected to be a virgin before marriage and faithful to her husband after. Men were permitted concubines as long as they could afford to keep them and the legitimate wife was not particularly jealous, because her social status was higher than that of the concubine.

This is typical of the pattern seen in the vast majority of societies of the past. Men occupied nearly all the positions of political power, and those that held the highest rank in society gained access to the most females. Mythical societies like the Amazons, which are supposed to have reversed this pattern, are purely imaginary; they never existed (Goldberg, 1977).

Among human societies, polygyny is by far the most common marital system (Ford and Beach, 1951). George Murdock's (1967) *Ethnographic Atlas* presents a categorization of 849 societies. Of these, 709 are polygynous and only four are polyandrous (women being permitted more than one husband). In the latter, exceptional cases, extreme conditions can usually be identified, such as severe economic deprivation leading to the practice of female infanticide. The surplus of males and the need to have more than one bread-winner thus creates a climate in which it is acceptable for women to acquire more than one husband. Even then, the women seem little inclined to capitalize on their privilege.

As noted above, in officially monogamous societies like our own, men are usually recognized as being more attracted to the idea of extra-marital sex than women, and many socially powerful men maintain mistresses as well as legal wives. Oil millionaire Paul Getty Senior, for example, kept a house full of women who were effectively wives. The practice of 'serial polygamy', of marrying a succession of wives one after another, is also more common among rich and powerful men in our society, such as Hollywood film stars like Charlie Chaplin and Micky Rooney.

Officially acknowledged polygamy is a much more widespread norm. Throughout the world it is common for women to be treated as the property of their husbands. In cultures as far removed from one another as the Aboriginals of Australia and the Eskimos of Alaska, wives may be bought and sold, inherited, loaned to guests and friends and used to pay debts. The number of wives a man has is determined primarily by how many he can afford to support (Mulder, 1988).

Similarly, in all societies prostitution is an almost exclusively female occupation, sex being viewed as a service that is rendered to men by women. The few male prostitutes that do exist cater mostly to homosexual men and are called 'rent boys'; gigolos are an extremely rare breed and their services as escorts, companions and status symbols are just as important as their stud value.

The treatment of women as sexual commodities is dictated not just by the superior social power of men but by the simple biological fact that the reproductive potential of a man is much greater than that of a woman. For example, the late King Sobhuza II of Swaziland had more than a hundred wives, around six hundred children and untold numbers of grandchildren. In fact, about 20 per cent of Swazis are said to be members of his family. It hardly needs to be said that no woman can ever produce anything remotely like six hundred children, regardless of how many husbands she acquires or men she sleeps with. Despite Catherine the Great's reputation for lustiness, and for having sex with vast numbers of men about the court, she was not distinguished as a prolific mother.

The *Guinness Book of Records* lists sixty-nine as the greatest number of children ever produced by a woman, compared with an official male record of 888 contributed by the last Sharatan Emperor of Morocco. Had he been inclined towards monogamy, his genes would have been much rarer in the world today.

This fundamental physiological difference between mammalian males and females must, throughout history, have led to divergences between the sexual instincts of the two genders. To say that King Sobhuza and the Moroccan Emperor are exceptional men is irrelevant; the point is that men who are exceptional in exactly this respect pass more of their genes on to the next generation of men than do ordinary men. And, however slight this tendency, it is bound to have a cumulative effect on the evolution of male instincts over a period of several million years. For women, what counts is that the survival of the limited number of children they do produce is assured, and this depends on the *quality* of the progenitors, not their quantity. Thus women will inevitably have evolved different instincts from those of men – tendencies toward partner selectivity and loyalty as mothers, not lust and sexual sensational-seeking.

Variations in permissiveness

Cultures do show considerable differences with respect to overall levels of permissiveness (Broude, 1976). Modern Western society is reasonably tolerant about sexual exploration, adultery, divorce and variations like homosexuality. This may be attributed to a number of factors including geographical mobility, urban anonymity and effective contraception. Other societies, such as Japan, are much more 'traditional' or puritanical overall, with attitudes more like those that prevailed in Europe during Victorian times. With the advent of AIDS there are signs that in Western societies now the pendulum is beginning to swing back from its peak of permissiveness in the 1970s.

Despite such variations in attitude, the same sex differences may always be observed. In research on Japanese social attitudes, for example, Wilson and Iwawaki (1980) found that, despite a more puritanical climate of opinion overall, men took a fairly relaxed attitude towards sexually permissive issues such as strip-tease, pornography, divorce and 'casual living', while women generally favoured social order and restraint, as indicated by their endorsement of concepts like patriotism, moral education, Church authority, censorship, chaperons and chastity. This pattern is consistent with that found in our own society and all others that have so far been empirically studied. Women of all cultures emerge as more caring, religious, traditional and opposed to hedonism than men.

It is interesting to note that, although women were more likely to endorse the two women's liberation items in the Wilson–Patterson Attitude Inventory that was used (women judges and working mothers), men were marginally more in favour of birth control and abortion. The same is true of Western society and gives the lie to the argument of certain feminists that it is men who force women into having babies against their will. If birth control and abortion are feminist issues, they actually receive more support from men than from women, even though in the case of men these attitudes may be motivated more by hedonism than idealism.

A similar picture emerges with respect to sexual fantasies in Japan compared with Britain (Iwawaki and Wilson, 1983). In both countries men report much higher levels of fantasizing overall, a greater number of active rather than passive fantasies (i.e. doing things rather than having things done to them) and more impersonal fantasies (e.g. fetishism, voyeurism, use of objects for stimulation) than sado-masochistic ones (e.g. whipping and spanking). For women, the reverse is true in both the Western and oriental cultures.

The theory of cultural determinism

Curiously, cross-cultural data are often cited by feminists as supporting their point of view that sex roles are socially learned. Most frequently they refer to a very influential book written many years ago by Margaret Mead called *Sex and Temperament in Three Primitive Societies* (1935). In this book Mead compared the sex roles of three New Guinea Societies, and claimed that all three were arranged very differently from our own. In the Arapesh culture both men and women were supposed to be mild-mannered and lacking in libido (rather like European women); in the Mundugumor both genders seemed aggressive and high sexed ('masculine'); while the Tchambuli supposedly showed a reversal of European sex roles, with the women being dominant and the men emotionally dependent. At the time, Mead concluded that 'all personality traits that we label masculine or feminine are as lightly linked to sex as are the clothing, the manners and the form of head-dress that a society at a given period assigns to either sex'.

This statement of cultural determinism has been widely quoted in favour of the idea that sex roles are infinitely malleable and is perhaps more responsible than almost any other source for the extreme environmentalism from which American psychology is only recently beginning to recover. However, a detailed look at Mead's own data does not support these conclusions. For example, as part of his initiation the Tchambuli boy was required to kill a victim and hang the head in the ceremonial house as a trophy. It is hard to see how this behaviour could be called effeminate. Likewise, among the 'mild-mannered' Arapesh the men, but not the women, were head-hunters before the advent of European civilization and most of the child-rearing was done by women.

Dr Mead has since conceded that her conclusions were to some extent unjustified and exaggerated. In reviewing Goldberg's (1977) book *The Inevitability of Patriarchy*, she says: 'It is true that all the claims so glibly made about societies led by women are nonsense. . . . Men have always been the leaders in public affairs and the final authorities at home' (*Redbook*, October 1983,

p. 38). The problem is that early anthropologists were so impressed by the differences they observed among cultures that they failed to document some of the equally important uniformities. In this sense anthropologists are like any tourists, only noticing the way in which the holiday country is different from home. Cultural determination may apply to overall levels of permissiveness within a culture and some superficial expressions of sexuality, but the basic structure of sex roles is fairly universal.

Another of Mead's books, *Coming of Age in Samoa* (1929), which is also widely cited in support of 'cultural determinism', has also been shown to be untrue in all its central conclusions (Freeman, 1983). In this book, Mead identified Samoa as a pacific paradise, peaceful, free from religious conflict and enjoying a system of free love, devoid of jealousy and rape. In fact, as Freeman shows, the Samoans are highly competitive, devoutly religious, place a high value on chastity and have a rape rate about two and a half times that of the United States. Freeman presents evidence that things were probably much the same in the 1920s when Mead was doing her field-work and he accuses her of naively selecting anecdotes to support her environmentalist bias. Mead became one of the most famous anthropologists in America because her findings suited the political climate of the day. Unfortunately they were little more than a mixture of self-deception, falsehood and fantasy.

This brief review of animal and cross-cultural evidence was intended to show that the gender roles and stereotypes that are observed in our society are consistent with sex differences displayed by the vast majority of other species and societies. It is therefore misleading to attribute such differences to patterns of upbringing unique to Western society. If its masculine and feminine stereotypes were arrived at by some accidental social decision, then the same 'accident' has occurred in virtually every other society, animal and human, that has ever been known; a coincidence rather too remarkable to be countenanced seriously.

4 · *Can the Differences Be Suppressed?*

In previous chapters I have presented evidence that there are substantial differences between men and women with respect to psychological as well as physical attributes, and that these differences are better accounted for by evolutionary theory than by social learning theory. A third, separate issue concerns the ease with which these differences could be overridden by appropriate social and political manipulation. Even though no society in the past seems to have managed to produce a reversal of sex roles, or even an identity of roles, this is not necessarily to say that such a state of affairs could not be achieved in the future.

As a matter of fact some people believe that Western society is changing under the influence of the women's movement in a way that promises to abolish male–female differences in the near future. This seems to be the thrust of the argument raised by some critics who state that what I say about sex differences was true in the past but is no longer relevant in modern society. According to this point of view, enormous strides have been made by women towards political and economic equality, and psychological gender differences have all but disappeared in the wake of this movement. Such as argument seems to contradict the other frequently voiced position which holds that observed gender differences are due to the peculiar conditions prevailing in society. This would seem to imply that other cultures and past societies are more favourable to gender role identity than is Western society today; but we shall let this contradiction pass for the moment.

Suppose we accept the proposition that social attitudes have changed (which seems quite reasonable) and that modern Western society has been making attempts to diminish the power of sex-role stereotypes. Certainly it is true to say that the feminist position has had many very eloquent spokeswomen (and men) over the past two decades. Numerous books and articles have been produced which preach that women should be more like men, that men should be more like women and that society should promote equality and identity as far as possible. Bookstalls are crammed with 'women's consciousness' materials, many of which have become best-sellers; there are college courses, particularly in the United States, which are devoted to 'women's studies'; children's books are vetted for 'sexist' language and assumptions, and there are prominent feminists in all branches of the media.

All of this would seem to give women in our society much greater opportunity to exercise freedom of choice with respect to their sexual and romantic behaviour, at least compared with the range of possibilities that were open to previous generations. This being the case, if men and women really are similarly inclined by nature, we might expect to find the age-old double standard of sexual morality breaking down to some extent. The new generation of young women should be seeking sexual thrills in a manner usually attributed to the male stereotype.

Whether or not the women's movement could result in males shifting towards the traditionally feminine attitude of monogamous devotion is more open to argument, since most feminists appear to think the male life-style is the one that both sexes would naturally prefer and gravitate towards if things were truly equal. Feminists are surely motivated more by envy of male privileges than sympathy for the male lot.

How much have attitudes changed?

An opportunity to investigate the question of changes in sexual inclinations arose when I was asked to supervise a large-scale sex survey by the *Sun*, Britain's best-selling daily newspaper. A questionnaire covering many areas of sexual attitudes and behaviour was issued as a pull-out section in the paper and readers were invited to complete it and return it by past. After discarding any that did not appear to have been completed properly, 4,767 questionnaires were submitted to computer analysis (Wilson, 1981b). Although the female sample was larger (about three women returning questionnaires to every two men), males and females were fairly comparable on major demographic indices and were reasonably representative of the adult population of Britain as regards occupational status.

In order that today's generation of women could be compared with their mothers, the sample was divided into two broad age-groups below and above the age of thirty. This was an arbitrary division, chosen as a round number which happened to split the total sample roughly in half. The average age of the under-thirties was twenty-three and that of the over-thirties was forty. Thus we obtained two generations who presumably grew up in different social climates with respect to the issues of women's liberation.

Of the many questions asked, three were particularly pertinent to the issue of the 'double standard' of sexual behaviour. The first concerned the number of different sex partners that had been experienced in the course of their lifetime. Men claimed to have had sexual intercourse with about twice as many different partners as women. This difference was no more marked in the older generation than the younger one. Since the older generation had had more time to accumulate experience with a variety of different partners, these figures could be read as indicating that the younger age-group is showing signs of being more adventurous overall. Nevertheless, the gender difference remains the same.

Incidentally, this sex difference might prompt the reader to ask where the men find the supply of extra partners that enables them to raise their 'variety' scores so far beyond those of women. One answer is that a small minority of highly active women (some of them professional prostitutes) cater for the male novelty-seeking urge, while the rest conduct their sex lives with relative reserve and decorum. This corresponds to the old idea that there as two types of women – those for pleasure and those for marrying.

There may be some truth in this proposition, but variations in the way the question was answered, for instance differing definitions of the term 'partner', may account for some of the difference. Women may enumerate relationships only, conveniently forgetting about casual sexual encounters because 'they don't count', whereas men are totalling 'belt notches'. Also, the preponderance of male over female homosexuality may have something to do with it; some of the sex partners claimed by men might be other men.

Whatever its origin, this gender difference does not seem to have diminished in the present generation of young people. Even if the figures only represent a tendency for men to boast and women to be modest, it is interesting that no change has occurred in recent years.

The second question in the survey that is relevant to the present discussion concerned the readiness with which members of each gender would be prepared to enter into sexual relationships with new partners. Men were about three times as likely as women to seek sex 'at the first possible opportunity', while women were three times as likely to prefer to wait until there is 'some commitment to a steady relationship'. Here, again, there was not the slightest hint within the data that the gender differences diminished in younger people in relation to the older generation. In fact, the similarity of the results from one age-group to the next was nothing short of remarkable, the percentages falling within each response category being virtually identical (see Table 4).

Another question asked people whether or not they were satisfied with their love-lives and, if not, how they would like them changed (see Table 3). Men were slightly more frustrated than women and, as expected, dissatisfied men were much more inclined towards experiencing variety in their partners and exciting variations on the sex act, while those women who were dissatisfied wanted more sex with their current spouse or steady partner. Again, there was no detectable difference between the older and younger generations with respect to these preferences.

Table 4 Willingness of British men and women to engage in
sexual intercourse at various phases of a new
relationship (in percentages)

Age	Male (N = 1,862)		Female (N = 2,905)	
	<30	>30	<30	>30
The first moment you can	38	32	9	9
When you have got to know them a little better	44	40	44	36
Not until there is some commitment to a steady relationship	8	8	25	28
Not outside marriage	10	18	18	22

Source: Wilson, 1981b.

Young men remain preoccupied with variety and excitement,
while young women still want a lot of sex with the men they
love.

The results of this survey constitute further support for the
evolutionary theory of gender differences underlying the
ubiquitous 'double standard'. The remarkable consistency in
answers to the questions from one age-group to another suggests
that gender differences in sexual attitudes and behaviour had
not changed much over two decades of active feminism and
were presumably therefore not easily modified by media
propaganda. This appears to be so, even though, as we have
said, cultures are known to shift as a whole from puritanism to
permissiveness.

Some cross-generational studies (Curran, 1975; King, Balswick
and Robinson, 1977) show that modern young women are more
likely to experience pre-marital intercourse than their mothers
and that society as a whole is becoming more tolerant of non-
marital sex. They do not, however, point to any appreciable
collapse in the instincts underlying gender differences in mating
behaviour in the wake of all the publicity accorded to feminist

theories and ideals. Any slight 'convergence of standards' that may have been observed by these researchers is probably confined to the university campuses from which they drew their subjects.

A key question

Recently, Symons and Ellis (1988) checked on the continuing reality of male–female differences in desire for partner novelty, using a question that was designed on socio-biological principles to yield maximum separation of the sexes: 'If the opportunity presented itself to have sexual intercourse with an anonymous member of the opposite sex who was as competent a lover as your partner but no more so, and who was as physically attractive as your partner but no more so, and there was *no* risk of pregnancy, discovery or disease, and no chance of forming a more durable relationship, do you think you would do so?' When this question was put to 232 female and 183 male education students in California, nearly half of the men said they certainly or probably would, as against 17 per cent of the women.

Symons and Ellis then proceeded to alter the details of the question so as to vary the attractiveness of the new partner and the possibilities of a long-term relationship developing out of it. By this technique, male interest was found to be influenced by physical attractiveness but not by the chances of a long-term relationship. Female sexual interest was not enhanced by increases in physical attractiveness of the prospective partner, but it was affected by details which referred to opportunities for a permanent relationship. These data show that even in modern-day California gender differences with respect to the desire for partner novelty remain quite striking.

In presenting evidence that modern women have changed little with respect to attitudes and behaviour, I do not mean to suggest that the women's movement has been totally impotent. Considerable advances have been made towards equality of *opportunity* in educational, occupational and economic spheres which most people would heartily applaud. Women nowadays are less likely to feel confused or guilty about being atypical of their sex-role stereotype. If they feel inclined to pursue an occupation that was previously the preserve of men, for example, law, engineering or medicine, they no doubt feel much more free to do so these days. Likewise, women who have the same sexual proclivities as men probably feel more comfortable in today's social climate about admitting and exercising them. All this, most people would agree, is to the good.

The feminist movement only becomes unreasonable, in my opinion, when scientific evidence is denied because it is politically discomforting or when women who would otherwise have been contented wives and mothers are induced to think of themselves as inferior because they have not pursued careers outside the home.

Regression in the kibbutz

Attempts to achieve sexual equality are not unique to present-day Anglo-American society. A brave and fascinating experiment in women's liberation was conducted by the Israelis when they set up their rural communes, the kibbutzim, during the colonization of Palestine in the early part of this century. A central part of their semi-Marxist ideology was the total emancipation of women from all inequalities (sexual, social, economic and intellectual) that had been imposed upon them by traditional society.

According to Israeli Utopian theory, the burden of child-rearing and home-making was the root cause of sex-role differentiation and female inequality. Therefore radical changes in family structure were instituted. Traditional marriage was replaced by a system of cohabitation in which a man and woman were assigned shared sleeping accommodation within the commune but retained their separate names and identities. The children were removed from special contact with their parents and reared with others of the same age in community-run nurseries where they played, ate, slept and were educated. Adults were supposed to think of all the kibbutz children as joint social property and were discouraged from developing particularly close relationships with their own offspring.

Thus freed from the 'domestic yoke', women were expected to engage in agricultural and productive work to the same extent as men, and men were likewise expected to share in traditional female work. Classically feminine clothes, cosmetics, jewellery and hair-styles were rejected. In order to be equals of men, it was thought women would have to look like men as well as share traditionally male roles.

When anthropologists Melford and Audrey Spiro examined the achievements of the kibbutzim in 1950, the experiment appeared to have been largely successful and their preconception of human nature as 'culturally relative' was held to be confirmed. However, in 1975 Melford Spiro returned to the kibbutz for a follow-up study and was surprised to discover that in the intervening quarter-century striking changes had occurred in the domain of marriage, family and sex-roles which 'all but undid the earlier revolution' (Spiro, 1979). The younger generation of women, although raised with unisex models (women driving tractors and men in domestic service occupations) and taught from early childhood that men and women are the same in nature, were now pressing to be allowed fulfilment in the role of mother. 'Women's rights' had taken on almost exactly the reverse meaning to that in our society.

The kibbutz government had become predominantly male, apparently because the women showed little interest in politics, and a traditional division of labour along sexual lines had become established. Men were doing most of the productive work, while women were doing mostly community and service work such as teaching, nursing and housekeeping. Marriage had reverted to its original form, with a full wedding ceremony and celebration, and public displays of attachment and 'ownership', previously almost taboo, were now commonplace. The units of residence had changed from the group to the married couple, and couples were now claiming and gaining the 'right' to enjoy the company of their own children. Children slept with their own parents and spent a great deal more time with them. Women had also shown a return to traditional 'femininity' in terms of appearance, temperament (empathy and lack of assertiveness) and hobbies. 'In the one place where feminists thought their ideal existed, the feminine mystique is ripening as fast as the corn in the fields' (*New York Times*, April 1976).

This collapse in what had seemed to be a successful campaign to abolish gender differences might be explained in terms of exposure to outside – for example, city – influences, but on close examination Spiro found this explanation to be unsatisfactory. Studies of play preferences of kibbutz children revealed that the girls most often played 'mother' (bestowing care and affection on a doll or small animal), while the most common game played by boys was imitating animals (not the domestic animals with which they were familiar, but wild and ferocious animals like snakes and wolves). Social learning theory cannot easily explain why girls should adopt a culturally appropriate model (the parenting woman) in their fantasy play, while boys adopt a culturally irrelevant model (wild animals). Biological pre-dispositions towards nurturance and aggression in girls and boys respectively seems far more plausible as an explanation of this difference. A careful examination of evidence like this led Spiro to conclude that the sex-role counter-revolution that he had observed in the modern kibbutz represented a reassertion of nature, rather than conformity induced by reactionary social influences. For a person previously commited to 'cultural relativity theory', this was a considerable turn-about in attitude.

The first sign of a confrontation between nature and ideology in the kibbutz concerned the issue of public nudity. The ideological authorities had early on determined that sexual equality would best be promoted by disregarding all differences in male and female anatomy. Boys and girls in the children's houses were therefore raised in a theoretically 'sex-blind' atmosphere, using the same toilets and showers and dressing in front of each other. This worked perfectly well until the girls reached puberty, at which point (quite spontaneously and contrary to prevailing social attitudes) they developed intense feelings of embarrassment and began to demand privacy. The girls began to rebel actively against these mixed-sex arrangements, refusing to admit boys into the showers with them and undressing with the lights out, or in some private place. For some time the authorities refused to change the system but were eventually convinced that the discomfort of the girls was to be taken seriously, and today most kibbutz high schools have separate bathroom facilities for boys and girls.

Again, it is difficult to see how cultural influences could be held responsible for this failure of ideology. Why should shame associated with nudity strike selectively at pubescent girls and not at boys of the same age, or younger girls? The modesty that girls develop at puberty is apparently not due to social guilt induction; much more likely, it is an aspect of the female coyness which is biologically preprogrammed because it serves the mating strategy of high partner selectivity and general sexual reserve.

Teenage sexuality in the kibbutz

A survey of adolescent sexuality in the kibbutz conducted by Dr Helen Antonovsky (1980) is also revealing. She felt that the sexual behaviour of kibbutz teenagers would be particularly interesting, not only because prevailing ideology had stressed sexual equality for many years, but also because the kibbutz environment is extremely permissive. According to Antonovsky, contraception and abortion are readily available and there is easy access to potential partners without adult surveillance. Environmentalists might therefore be dismayed (and moralists relieved) to learn that even in this highly permissive climate less than half the girls had started engaging in sexual intercourse by the age of eighteen, and then it was nearly always with one particular boyfriend with whom they were in love. Clearly it takes more than social permission to interest most girls in casual sexual relations.

Comparing the kibbutz sample with adolescents raised in traditional Israeli society, Antonovsky found that certain superficial aspects of the double standard, for instance, the value put upon pre-marital virginity, were diminished. However, questions more crucial to an evolutionary theory of gender differentiation (that is, closer to that posed by Symons and Ellis above) showed no such change. For example, only half the boys, but nearly all the girls, thought love was an important prerequisite to coitus in both kibbutz and non-kibbutz samples. Similarly, about 12 per cent of boys as opposed to 2 per cent of girls said, 'It doesn't matter with whom one has coitus.' This was regardless of whether or not they had been reared in the kibbutz environment.

The elegance of socio-biological theory can be seen in its ability to predict which components of sexuality will be most resistant to cultural variations. Marriage is a social institution, the details of which vary enormously from one part of the world to another, but female selectiveness in choosing a mate is much more biologically determined and therefore more universal.

The decline of feminism

Although our own society has perhaps never reached the same degree of sex-role equality as that established in the early days of the Israeli kibbutz, there are signs over the last decade that a reaction has begun to develop against feminism within Anglo-American society. In 1980, for example, a group was established called the Campaign for the Feminine Woman, which is an organization of men and women dedicated to the downfall of feminism and a return to traditional sex roles. With the battle cry of *Vive la difference*, this group wages war against what they see as the erosion of feminine values and the damage done by crude attempts to enforce equality. The general secretary of CFW was a married woman called Deirdre Tucker, working in newspaper advertising out of economic necessity: 'There's nothing I'd like more than to stay at home and look after my husband and the family which I hope will come along one day. . . . I'm giving voice to feelings that I know are held by millions, and not just men. Feminine women don't have to be mindless and silly. Their role in life is different, but just as important.' Although this group did not declare its actual membership, they claimed to be 'beseiged' by support from all over the world and to have a growing following consisting of roughly equal numbers of men and women (*She* magazine, December 1980).

We have also seen an increasing number of articles by women journalists questioning the assumptions of feminism. For example, Mary Kenny wrote in the *Daily Express* (August 1980):

> Ten years ago I was a militant Women's Libber. But today I have to admit, I'm a changed person. . . . The endless questioning about why there aren't more women in top jobs simply ignores a fundamental reality: most women don't want top jobs because they want some time and space in their lives for their families. . . . Endlessly scolding women for not aspiring to top jobs simply makes those of us who are at home with our families feel inadequate and even guilty. . . . It implies that being a housewife is just 'going to waste' and that mothers would be better employed being tycoons or nuclear physicists. Such talk puts most women down and putting women down is what is wrong with so much feminism nowadays.

This point of view recalls the comments of one of the kibbutz women (Spiro, 1979). Asked why women seemed to prefer 'inferior' jobs, she replied that men's work is mostly concerned with 'things' and 'animals', while the occupations preferred by women are concerned with people. 'Which is more important?'

Even Betty Friedan, who is sometimes credited with having founded the feminist movement a few decades ago, seems to have had second thoughts about feminism in her mature years. In her most recent book *The Second Stage* (1982) she expresses concern that the 'feminine mystique' has in some quarters given way to an equally rigid 'feminist mystique', which simply replaces the old dissatisfactions with a new set of problems for women:

Listening to my own daughters and sons, and others of their generation whom I meet, lecturing at universities or professional conferences or feminist networks around the country and around the world, I sense something out of focus, going wrong, in the terms by which they are trying to live the equality we fought for.

From these daughters – getting older now, working so hard, determined not to be trapped as their mothers were, and expecting so much, taking for granted the opportunities we had to struggle for – I've begun to hear undertones of pain and puzzlement, a queasiness, an uneasiness, almost a bitterness that they hardly dare admit. As if with all those opportunities that we won for them, and envy them, how can they ask out loud certain questions, talk about certain other needs they aren't supposed to worry about – those old needs which shaped our lives, and trapped us, and against which we rebelled?

. . . this sense of battles won, only to be fought over again, of battles that should have been won according to all the rules, and yet are not, of battles that suddenly one does not really want to win, and the weariness of battle altogether – how many women feel it?

Betty Friedan goes on to give many examples of the conflicts and anxieties faced by women who have found it impossible in practice to reconcile their new-found independence and career prospects with their more basic needs for love, family and children. In reality it becomes impossible to 'juggle it all' and many women have been left with a feeling of failure because they could not be 'superwomen' and achieve fulfilment in all aspects of their lives simultaneously. Betty Friedan is not sure what the answer is, but she does suggest the time has come to revalue some of the traditional feminine needs which the feminist movement has frequently denied and to restore the wife/mother role as a legitimate and important option.

Considerable disaffection with feminism was also apparent in a survey of 1,500 women aged between twenty-five and forty-five that was conducted in April 1982 by *Options*, a fairly progressive British women's magazine. While 91 per cent said, 'We have much more freedom than our mothers' generation', 51 per cent felt that emancipation had 'taken some of the romance out of life' and 77 per cent said their 'first duty was to their husband and family'. Fifty-eight per cent blamed the women's movement for the high divorce rate and 44 per cent expected the pendulum to start swinging back towards the traditional feminine role. No less than 87 per cent expressed a dislike of 'women who band together as feminists', agreeing that 'it's up to individuals to make their own lives work', and 21 per cent felt that women's liberation had 'done more harm to women than good'. The vast majority of women also wanted to be sexually interesting and attractive to men and to establish a relationship with a man they could 'lean on if necessary'. One rather telling comment emerged from a group discussion: 'I know it contradicts what I believe about sharing everything, but I do like to be with someone more powerful than I . . . a knight in shining armour . . . someone who will kill the dragon for me . . . someone who will be responsible.' *Options* concluded, rather sweepingly, that 'inside every liberated woman is an old-fashioned girl'.

Another possible indication of a feminist decline is the recovery of traditional women's magazines from earlier circulation losses. A front runner in Britain is *Women's Weekly* which features knitting, gardening and household hints – a formula that has hardly changed since its beginnings in 1911. Also with a circulation in excess of one and a half million is *Woman*, which is similarly committed to the *kinder–kuche* (children and kitchen) formula. According to the editors of these magazines, traditional feminine values were never really lost but only suffered a slight set-back during the 'hysteria of the late sixties when women were encouraged to throw away their bras and often their husbands' (*Daily Telegraph*, June 1979). Some more liberated and trendy women's magazines such as *Cosmopolitan* have proved quite successful, but those which set out with the assumption that women would acquire interests directly parallel to those of men, for instance by printing nude male pin-ups, have failed dismally. *Nova*, which tried the experiment, soon folded, and *Playgirl* just survives with a high proportion of sales to men, some homosexual and some buying the magazine as a joke, present or titillation for their girlfriends.

Feminism as a form of puritanism

Even if feminism is not in decline, it seems to have shifted its emphasis in a manner that looks like a return to certain traditional female values. In particular, consider feminist attitudes towards sexual permissiveness and erotica. When women's liberation first took off in the 1960s, the thrust of the argument was that women should assume all the freedoms traditionally enjoyed by men, including casual, hedonistic sex – what Erica Jong called the pursuit of the 'zipless fuck'. Bras were burned and women were exhorted to abandon the shackles of the sexually restrictive upbringing that had rendered them 'female eunuchs'.

However, as we moved into the 1970s and 1980s women's liberation was progressively replaced by a more puritanical kind of 'feminism', which argued that, rather than emulating the sexual irresponsibility of men, women should insist that men curtail their baser instincts and stop treating women as sex objects. Hence we have campaigns to outlaw pin-ups in newspapers, attacks on beauty contests as 'meat markets' and lawsuits being brought against men for 'sexual harassment' at work. Feminists in Sweden have even called for the introduction of 'erotic-free zones' in the workplace in which women can 'take refuge from all the meaningful heavy glances and indecent suggestions' that they are normally subjected to. The first of such zones has recently been established at a hospital in Vasteras, a small industrial town west of Stockholm.

The interesting thing about this feminist-backed call for decency and censorship is that it is not only a return to Victorian values but it has much in common with Islamic principles that prevail in some of the Arab countries that are particularly repressive to women. Up until the 1960s beauty contests were an acceptable part of Egyptian life, but the revival of Islamic fundamentalism has led to problems for this kind of entertainment. After threats of bombing and acid-throwing at contestants, the 'Best Girl in Egypt' competition of 1988 had to be changed from a swimsuit parade to one in which the women wore evening-gowns. Feminist protesters are a familiar sight at Western beauty contests, but they probably would not think of themselves as trying to impose an Islamic-style *chador* upon women. Although feminism is usually regarded as a radical movement, it has strong components that are traditionally female, perhaps even 'chauvinistic'.

It appears, then, that some aspects of the woman's movement may already have passed their peak and that in Western society we are witnessing a slight swing of the pendulum back towards an appreciation of basic gender differences and Victorian values. It seems that in prescribing separate sex roles society creates a powerful equilibrium that is not easily shifted and that exhibits a strong tendency to revert to the status quo when it is dislodged. This is not to say that feminism has made no lasting changes in society, but the simple-minded belief that men and women can easily be induced to think, feel and behave in a manner identical with one another is revealed as misguided.

5 · *Sexual Anomalies and Difficulties*

It is within the area of sexual and mating behaviour itself that we expect to see the most striking differences between men and women. Just as some of the most outstanding physical differences between the genders are concerned with reproductive functions, so too the evolutionary view supposes that the instincts and inclinations within the spheres of love and sex will show the greatest divergence. In previous chapters I have sketched some of the evidence that men are more readily aroused sexually, more willing to enter into casual sexual relationships and generally more adventure-seeking in their sexual preferences. Here I hope to show that an evolutionary theory of sex differences can illuminate a number of sexual anomalies and problems that might hitherto have seemed puzzling, as well as drawing further support from their investigation.

Intersexual conditions

The division of people into categories of male and female is only a convenient fiction. It is more true in some respects to think in terms of degrees of maleness. All foetuses develop along female lines unless there are hormonal instructions to alter the individual in the direction of masculinity. This normally happens if the chromosome pattern is the typically male (XY) one or includes at least one Y, but it does not always occur, and the masculinization may be incomplete.

73

At puberty the vocal cords of most boys double in length and their voices change from soprano to baritone. However, in a small proportion of boys this 'break' is incomplete and the pitch change is arrested at a point half-way between the typical male and female voices. Such men may become highly prized as operatic tenors, but there is an increased likelihood that they will be shorter than average, lower in sex drive and 'hysterical' in personality (Wilson, 1984; Chapter 2). In an even smaller proportion of men the pitch of the voice does not alter at all, although it gains in strength and maturity. Such men are called counter-tenors, and they have been so prized in church music in the past that their numbers were artificially boosted (castrati). Higher-voiced men are not necessarily effeminate in all respects, but the varying degree of voice modification following puberty provides an example of the fact that masculinization processes are not absolute for all organs and individuals.

In some 'men' the body organs seem to be largely insensitive to the effects of male hormones, with the result that they do not 'take'. This is called the androgen insensitivity syndrome (or sometimes 'testicular feminization'). The individuals concerned, although genetic males, appear as females with soft skin and well-developed breasts. They are infertile, having internal testicles and no uterus, and are usually not recognized as males until menstruation fails to appear during adolescence.

American endocrinologist R. B. Greenblat (1981) has suggested that Joan of Arc may have been a case of androgen insensitivity, since there are historical indications that she did not menstruate and had no pubic hair even at the age of nineteen (both typical manifestations of the syndrome). If this were so, and it is unlikely we shall ever know for sure, it might help to explain her penchant for dressing in men's clothes and her male-like aspirations to military leadership. However, psychological studies of such people do not suggest that male behaviour and interests are features of this syndrome (Ellis and Ames, 1987), which rather weakens Greenblat's case.

On the other side of the coin, there are genetic (XX) females who are masculinized to a greater or lesser extent; for example, those whose adrenal cortex produces an unusually high amount of androgen (male hormone). This is known as the adrenogenital syndrome. Such women may have an enlarged clitoris, enhanced sex drive and a tendency towards 'tomboyism' in their interests and life-style (Money and Ehrhardt, 1972). At the extreme, they are physically and mentally indistinguishable from men, although they are obviously not able to father children (nor usually to mother them).

Then there are individuals who are a genetic mixture of male and female, having an XXY chromosome pattern. This is called Klinefelter's syndrome, and affected individuals tend to have small male organs, some breast development and low libido (Katchadourian and Lunde, 1975).

Finally, there are 'supermales' with a double dose of Y chromosome (XYY), who are often very tall and masculine-looking and who are over-represented among those prisoners who have committed violent and sexual crimes (see Chapter 7).

Many more intersexual conditions could be listed, but the point is that no watertight definition exists of who is male and who is female. This is particularly problematic in the field of athletics where there is of course a very considerable difference between the average performance of men and women. Until recent decades, when a chromosome test of gender was introduced to international athletics, it was estimated that a very high proportion of female records were held by women with male chromosomes, who would now be classified as men. But the chromosome test is also inadequate, because it is entirely possible for a genetic female sufficiently exposed to male hormones to end up as masculine as Burt Reynolds.

This is more than a technical quibble. The transsexual tennis player Renée Richards, who has coached some of the top players in the world, was not ranked at all as a man but was such a threat to female competitors that she had to be banned from competing with them on the basis of her male chromosomes. Again, the femininity of some top women tennis players is an interesting matter of conjecture, since a high proportion (perhaps as many as half) are said to be lesbian in their sexual preference. Of course there is no reason to suppose they have male chromosomes, but their sex orientation is a clue to the likelihood that their hormone balance was tilted in the male direction at some time during development. Consistent with this argument is the finding that some lesbian women have unusually high testosterone levels (Meyer-Bahlburg, 1979).

There is evidence that women who are successful in competition with men in the business world are more like men in anatomy and patterns of circulating hormones than are traditional, domestic women (see Chapter 6), and it could be argued that in order to compete successfully with men in some spheres women need to be or become like men to some extent. Writers who point to the closing gap betwen male and female athletic records as a sign of increased equality (e.g. Nicholson, 1984) seem to have missed this point. Records are held by exceptional women, while the gap in *average* performance between men and women in physical sports remains much the same. Since there is no satisfactory way of determining who is, and who is not, a legitimate female for athletic purposes, records for women are bound to be somewhat arbitrary. They are likely to be broken whenever a somewhat masculinized women slips through the qualification procedure.

The sex identity of hermaphrodites

Research by John Money and others over the past few decades has shown that when a child is born hermaphroditic (of indeterminate sex) but is decisively identified as one sex or the other by doctors and parents from a very early age, that child will usually be fairly accepting of the assigned gender and the social role that accompanies it (Money and Ehrhardt, 1972). This fact has been quoted by many social learning theories as support for their position that sex roles are acquired rather than inborn. If a child is genetically one sex but can successfully be reared as a number of the other, they say, this must indicate the overwhelming power of social learning experiences. It is important, however, to recall in this connection that the biological factor determining gender is not the chromosome pattern but the balance of hormones to which the body and brain is exposed from conception onwards. An infant whose external genitalia are ambiguous is clearly only part masculinized and therefore genuinely intermediate in terms of gender, regardless of chromosome pattern. It is understandable that in cases like these it is possible to push the individual's identification towards one gender or the other with a combination of surgical and hormonal treatment and social persuasion, so that they are unlikely to dispute their assigned gender. This tells us nothing about the difficulties that would be encountered in trying to cross-socialize an individual of unambiguous sex without the aid of surgery or hormones. Money and his colleagues now recognize this distinction and no longer maintain the radical environmentalist viewpoint that is often quoted from their earlier papers.

In any case Money's early conclusions related specifically to gender *identity*, not the broader aspects of masculinity and femininity which are under partly separate brain control, being laid down in different areas of the brain and at different phases of pre-natal development (Ellis and Ames, 1987). Many of the androgenital cases, for example, identified themselves as women happily enough but showed distinct 'tomboyism' in their pattern of interests. They enjoyed 'rough-and-tumble' activities, preferred wearing trousers to dresses and were uninterested in marriage and motherhood.

Since Money's early work on hermaphroditism in humans, a fascinating new condition has come to light as a result of its prevalence within a particular mountain district of the Dominican Republic. Male pseudo-hermaphroditism (Imperato-McGinley *et al.*, 1974) or *machihembra* ('man-woman' as the locals call it) is an inherited enzyme deficiency which causes genetic males to develop as females until puberty, at which time androgen production is suddenly increased and the individual turns into a male (complete with penis, descended testicles, deep voice, facial and body hair and well-developed muscles). The interesting thing about these individuals is that, although raised as girls, they have little difficulty in adjusting to a male identity after their bodily conversion at puberty. They develop male mannerisms and attitudes and are sexually attracted to females just like normal men. Perhaps most interesting of all is the discovery that they often begin to think of themselves as boys at the age of five or six, well before any physical changes have begun to take place.

This may be regarded as one of the most direct tests of the relative power of society and hormones in determining gender identity and sex-role characteristics, and the hormones appear victorious. It should encourage us to listen sympathetically to the claims of transsexuals that they are 'trapped in the wrong body', for this is exactly the subjective experience of the pseudo-hermaphrodite, who is more fortunate in that subsequent proof (and a natural change) is provided.

Homosexuality and the brain

Apart from the constitutional anomalies outlined above, there are many people who seem to be physically normal representatives of one sex or the other but who prefer sexual contact with members of their own sex. Increased tolerance of this behaviour in recent decades has led some people to argue that no theoretical explanation of homosexuality is called for, any more than one needs to 'explain' heterosexuality. To the evolutionary theorist this is nonsense; heterosexuality has obvious survival benefits while homosexuality does not, so the latter is bound to arouse more scientific curiosity and demand special explanation.

A popular biological theory says that, during the process of masculinization of the developing male, some critical nuclei in the brain that are concerned with sexual preference somehow escape exposure to the circulating male hormone and the sex-target 'switch' is therefore not reset in the male direction (Feldman and MacCulloch, 1971). This leaves us with an individual who is male in body but female in sexual preference. Less commonly, the theory supposes, this sex-target switch gets accidentally masculinized in a constitutional female who otherwise remains normal, thus yielding a lesbian.

The strength of this hypothesis is shown in a recent review of research by Ellis and Ames (1987), although the effect of pre-natal sex hormones is probably more complex than that stated above. Apart from a masculinizing process that is largely under the control of foetal testosterone, we may have to recognize some separate feminizing effects upon the brain under the control of female hormones, especially luteinizing hormone (LH). This means that people can be more or less feminine, as well as more or less masculine, these two dimensions yielding a wider array of sexual types.

In addition, it is necessary to separate brain settings for sex orientation from brain settings for sex-typical behaviour. It is possible, for example, to have an individual who is macho both in body and personality but who prefers male sex partners, or vice versa. This is because the masculinization/feminization effects occur in different parts of the brain and, more importantly, at different times during pre-natal development. Indications are that sex orientation in humans depends critically upon the hormone balance prevailing during the third and fourth months of pregnancy, while secondary sex character-istics and sex-typical behaviour patterns are influenced more by hormones circulating during the fifth and sixth months of pregnancy. If the hormone balance changes from one phase of foetal development to the next, inconsistencies between sexual orientation and sex-role behaviour may be observed. Sex orientation is fixed relatively early in the old 'limbic' part of the brain, whereas sex-role behaviours are laid down later on in pregnancy in more diverse, 'newer' parts of the brain.

Ellis and Ames go on to review an impressive body of animal and human research which establishes pretty much beyond doubt that what we call homosexuality (an inversion of the normal relationship between body type and sexual orientation) may be created by five different procedures:

1 Direct alteration of hormones (by injection or castration) during foetal development
2 Using drugs to block or augment the effects of androgens. The list of drugs which may at least partially divert masculinization of the brain include Depo-Provera, cypro-terone acetate, barbiturates, diazepam and marijuana.

3 Exposure of the mother to severe emotional stress. Stress hormones carried in the mother's blood may cross the placenta and interfere with testosterone production in the baby.

4 In some circumstances the immune system may react against the biochemicals necessary for sexual differentiation, identifying them as foreign substances and attacking with antibodies that destroy them. Ultimately this can also reverse scx orientation.

5 Raising young animals in isolation from the opposite sex also impedes heterosexual adaptation, though the problem may be one of social skill and confidence rather than sex orientation as such.

Dominance and paraphilia

There seems little doubt that sexual preferences are partly determined by hormones before birth and, since there are more opportunities for something to 'go wrong' in the process of converting the standard female embryo into a sexually competent male, this helps to explain why male homosexuality is more common than lesbianism. But there are other possible reasons for the preponderance of male homosexuality, as well as other sex deviations (the paraphilias) which make use of the concept of the 'dominance hierarchy' (which, incidentally, depends itself largely on the second phase of brain masculinization).

As already noted, males are thrown into intense competition with one another for access to females and, since those that are successful monopolize more than one female, there is certain to be a great deal of redundant male libido. Various substitutes are therefore adopted to accommodate this excess libido, homosexual behaviour being one of the most common. In this view, the established genetic basis of homosexuality (Kallmann, 1952) is presumed to be non-specific, in fact much the same as that underlying the personality dimension of dominance versus submission. Men who are genetically less advantaged in social competition, whose pre-natal masculinization was incomplete or who perceive women as unapproachable as a result of some learning experience, are more prone to homosexual outlets. Although environmental influences are acknowledged, this dominance–failure theory is clearly not the same as a simple social learning or modelling theory of homosexuality. Copying others may occur as part of the process of developing a homosexual identity but is not in itself sufficient to account for it.

When two or more males compete for dominance within a hierarchy, biochemical changes take place following the outcome, such that the victor is prepared for sexual activity and the losers fall into a state of relative depression that may be basic to some forms of male sexual inadequacy (Rose, Bernstein and Gordon, 1975; McGuire, Raleigh and Johnson, 1983). Indeed, a loss of sexual appetite is often noted in depressive patients, and many of the conditions that predispose to depression can be viewed as representing a fall in social status and self-esteem (Hill, 1968).

Depression is understandably treated as an illness, but it could derive from circumstances in which a male finds he has to withdraw from a losing battle at least in the short term, so he lives to compete (and possibly reproduce) another day. The fact that men have a capacity to 'turn off' libido when faced with long periods of deprivation is evidenced by a decline in sexual fantasy, possibly connected with declining testosterone secretion, in men who are imprisoned or in hospital (Wilson, 1978).

Assuming that sex drive is not dissipated entirely following defeat, what other adaptations are possible? One of the most obvious is masturbation – a partial solution that is very widely employed. (Women sometimes masturbate but for different reasons than those of men – usually because they are short of orgasms, not potential partners.) The term 'wanker' carries the connotation that a man is inadequate to the task of obtaining women. Masturbation provides short-term relief but does not provide optimal sensation and lacks the important interpersonal element. Therefore, some men elaborate with fantasy-like partial experiences, such as looking at pornography, peeping at lovers in the park or women undressing in bedroom windows, exposing themselves to schoolgirls, rubbing up against women in crowds, or seeking contact with symbolic or conditioned associations of womanhood such as high-heeled shoes, underwear or 'motherly' discipline.

A dominance–failure interpretation of fetishism is supported by the work of La Torre (1980), who found that ego-deflatory feedback to male students, leading them to believe that women found them unattractive, diminished their interest in women as such, while at the same time increasing their response to impersonal female symbols such as shoes and underwear. Also consistent with this interpretation is the work of Gosselin and Wilson (1980) and Wilson and Cox (1983) showing that most types of sexually deviant men tend towards shyness and introversion to a degree that could impede the development of heterosexual capability.

Another solution to the problem of inter-male competition is to opt out and assume certain aspects of the female role. Many masochists, transvestites and transsexuals say they feel 'more relaxed' when assuming a submissive, feminine role (Gosselin and Eysenck, 1980); these behaviours may provide relief from the pressure of striving for masculine dominance.

There are plenty of animal models for such an adaptation. A species of fish that lives in the coral reefs of the Pacific changes sex according to its position in the dominance hierarchy. Social groups consist of one male and a harem of females occupying a particular territory, and the male suppresses any tendency of his females to change sex by aggressively dominating them. When he dies, however, the dominant female in the group promptly turns into a male and takes over the harem (Robertson, 1972).

Much of the homosexual behaviour that occurs among animals in the wild appears to be dominance related. In one species of tree lizard, mature males maintain territories containing several females. Smaller males may copulate with the females of the harem, but if a larger male comes around they must themselves assume the female role in copulation (Trivers, 1976). Inter-male battles in mountain sheep often end with the loser being mounted by the victor (Geist, 1971) and male monkeys use the female presentation position as a gesture of acquiescence to a superior male (Eibl-Eibesfeldt, 1971).

Not all human homosexuality can be explained in these terms, but certain kinds, especially that occurring in all-male environments such as prisons, public schools, ships and monasteries, often has such overtones. In the Arabian state of Oman, where women are virtually inaccessible outside of marriage, what is essentially a third gender has emerged. The *Xaniths*, as they are called, are biological males who dress differently from both men and women, use makeup and wear their hair longer than other men. They work in servile occupations and assume the submissive role in sexual relations with men (Wikan, 1977). Thus is a great deal of excess male libido released without female involvement.

There are many reasons why some men might feel unable to compete for women and find it easier to pursue sexual outlets in the gay community. They may have had unfortunate early encounters with women, causing them to feel incompetent or unattractive, or experienced savage punishment for heterosexual play in childhood. For whatever reason, these men decide to opt out of the heterosexual rat race and take their pleasure with others of their own gender.

The dominance–failure theory provides an additional explanation as to why homosexuality is so much more common in men than women (as indeed are most non-reproductive sexual variations such as fetishism, frotteurism, voyeurism, exhibitionism and bestiality). Although group selection theories are unfashionable, we may note that removing some males from the breeding pool does not affect group survival, since all the females can still be impregnated by the remaining males. In fact, it might even enhance species effectiveness by focusing breeding on males of higher 'stud value'. Deviant females do, however, represent a loss to the species, as well as to themselves, which is perhaps another reason why they are less common. Just as sexual reproduction may give a species an advantage over those that simply split in half, so inter-male competition may promote 'strength' within a species.

There is no reason to suppose that lesbians would be genetically disadvantaged in competition, but they could be slightly masculinized or defeminized by pre-natal hormone influences, or correspond with those male homosexuals who are disaffected with the opposite sex for other reasons (i.e. have learned to dislike them as a result of unpleasant contacts in the past). We have noted that lesbians are not so much lustful as love-seeking and, being naturally monogamous and affiliative, women may be preferred as sexual partners for their loyalty and faithfulness.

Somewhat crucial to the competition-difficulty hypothesis are studies of pairs of identical male twins where one twin is homosexual and the other heterosexual (Seward and Seward, 1980). Usually it is discovered that the homosexual twin has suffered some kind of illness in childhood which has retarded his physical and social development in relation to the heterosexual twin. This might restrict his exposure to girls and leave him with reduced confidence in his ability to attract and conduct sexual relationships with women. The dominance theory also puts a new slant on the frequently reported finding that male homosexuality and other sexual variations are associated with a weak father figure; the connection could be based on heredity rather than modelling. It is further consistent that male homosexuals have been shown to be less muscular in build and less self-confident than control males, whereas the same does not apply to lesbians.

The dominance theory may also help to explain why sado-masochistic practices such as slavery and humiliation are more common within gay male circles than the heterosexual population (Spengler, 1977; Kamel, 1980). Assuming that some degree of social dominance is necessary for adequate performance of the male sexual role (erection and insertion), heterosexuals have less of a problem because male dominance over females is fairly readily assumed. However, when two men are preparing for sexual activity, the matter of their relative dominance is more ambiguous, and so role-playing games such as master–slave, doctor–patient, headmaster–pupil or torturer–victim may be contrived to assist in the turn-on. Of course, many heterosexual couples also experiment with fantasy games of this kind, but they are seldom so preoccupied by them.

Also consistent with the dominance interpretation is the

discovery that fetishists, sado-masochists and transvestites share many common interests (Gosselin and Wilson, 1980). When male members of clubs catering to these three variations were surveyed with respect to their sexual fantasies and behaviour, there emerged a considerable degree of overlap among them. The outstanding common elements were enjoyment of impersonal sex objects such as clothing, instruments and materials (for example, 'being excited by rubber', 'wearing clothes belonging to the opposite sex') and the desire to take a submissive role in social and sexual encounters (for instance, 'being forced to do something', 'being tied up', 'being whipped or spanked'). In other words, the sexual interest of these men was directed either towards inanimate objects (where the issue of dominance does not arise) or towards a deliberate and decisive reversal of the normal dominance relationship so that they become childlike victims (thus avoiding the competitive struggle altogether).

Male sex targeting

Apart from competition/dominance difficulties, there is another reason why it is men and not women who become attached to unusual sex objects such as high-heeled shoes, small boys and disciplinarian women. Whereas female sexuality is relatively passive and responsive, males need to develop 'targets' for arousal, particularly in the form of visual configurations and verbal scenarios. This involves a certain amount of learning, some of which occurs very early in life (probably before the age of three) and is so inflexible that it may usefully be called 'imprinting' (Wilson, 1987b).

In many animals, such as guppies, crabs and ducks, the females seem to recognize the males by an inborn mechanism, but males have to learn how to find females (Daly and Wilson, 1979). Mistakes are often made, male butterflies being observed to court falling leaves and frogs mounting galoshes. Japanese quails raised by albino mothers are likely to want to mate with albino females in adulthood, and baboons raised in a zoo without access to females are likely to be sexually aroused by the keeper's gumboots (Epstein, 1987). The active, predatory, target-seeking nature of male sexuality thus constitutes another major reason why men are particularly prone to the distortions of sexual inclination that we call paraphilias.

It is probably no accident that the brain area responsible for assertive male sexuality is a part of the hypothalamus that is close to the visual input system (the preoptic nucleus). This could be connected with the well-known visual arousability of males, witnessed in the human case by sales of pornographic films and magazines and the fetishistic content of men's fantasies (see Chapter 1). Males are built to scan the environment for sexual objects; females, by contrast, are programmed to resist and escape from sexual encounters for a good part of the time.

Male and female homosexuality

This is not the place for a detailed evaluation of theories of homosexuality and sexual deviation. For present purposes, one major point to note is that the differing nature of the sexual inclinations of men and women can be seen in magnified form when placed in the context of homosexuality, where we are observing manifestations of elemental rather than compound gender. In homosexual behaviour we have a perfect testing ground for social and biological theories of sexuality. Here we can observe the behaviour of males and females in circumstances where there is no need to compromise with the proclivities of the opposite sex and where respect for social convention has already been largely forsworn.

What is seen is a strikingly different pattern of behaviour between male and female homosexuals. For one thing, gay men are a great deal more active sexually than lesbian women. Bell (1973) estimates that homosexual men have a partner turnover that is between ten and a hundred times greater than that of heterosexual men. About 25 per cent of homosexual males have sexual encounters with more than 1,000 partners (Bell, Weinberg and Hammersmith, 1981). Without the female brake on promiscuity, it seems, these men are able to indulge their novelty-seeking instinct with greater abandon. Lesbians, by contrast, show no such inclination towards exploratory sexuality; their sexual relationships tend to grow out of deep friendships and they are no more promiscuous in the course of their lifetime than are heterosexual women. Their median number of partners is only three (Loney, 1974). Of course, gay men have become less promiscuous in recent years as a result of knowledge about AIDS, but this is a fairly superficial restraint which tells us little about basic sexual desire.

A second finding that emerges from surveys of gay men is their emphasis on the visual characteristics of their partners (and potential new partners). Just like heterosexual men, they seek youth and beauty, some even to the extent of restricting themselves to pre-pubertal targets (Wilson and Cox, 1983). Lesbians, on the other hand, behave like heterosexual women in this respect, seeking long-term relationships based on personality qualities such as sympathy and loyalty more than physical appearance.

Male bisexuals and female bisexuals are also very different in their behaviour patterns (Blumstein and Schwartz, 1977). Bisexual men are frequently married and use other men (or boys) for casual sex and variety, rather in the same way men use prostitutes. Bisexual women seek long-term relationships with members of either sex and are more likely to alternate their partners than run them in parallel.

In men's prisons a great deal of homosexual behaviour occurs that centres around the need for sexual release and dominance within the power hierarchy. In women's prisons homosexual relationships are less common; when they do occur they appear to operate more as a quasi-kinship system, the women variously adopting the roles of wives, husbands, aunts and so on (Giallombardo, 1974).

These comparisons of 'free-running' sexual activity provide potent evidence for the argument that the inclinations of men and women are really quite different in nature. Freed from the need to behave in accordance with the restraints and expectations of the opposite sex, or society at large, male and female sexual divergence is magnified, the males seeking a variety of young, attractive partners and the females seeking stable, meaningful relationships with partners they can rely on emotionally.

Sexual responsiveness

If men are more readily aroused than women, they are also more easily satisfied. According to male folklore, 'There is only one thing more difficult than getting a woman started, and that is getting her stopped again.' The reason is that the sexual response cycle of women runs at a slower rate than that of men, so that on many occasions a woman will fail to reach orgasm before her partner is spent and ready for sleep. Depending on how close the woman gets to climax, this can be a very frustrating experience for her (although there is considerable variation of opinion among women as to whether sex without orgasm is pleasant or unpleasant – see Wallin, 1960). It is estimated that about one-third of women never experience orgasm during intercourse and another third do so only occasionally (Fisher, 1973).

Feminist explanations of this unfortunate state of affairs are usually presented in terms of male insensitivity as lovers. Chauvinism, they say, has been carried into the bedroom. If men were more gentle, patient and considerate in their love-making, the problem would disappear; instead they are selfish, brutish and too quick. Alternatively, women are sometimes recommended to try masturbation or lesbianism, in which the chances of orgasm are apparently greater (Hite, 1976).

There is no doubt an element of truth in this argument, although responsive and non-responsive women differ little in sexual techniques (Shope, 1968; Fisher, 1973). Nevertheless it tends to obscure a vital, relevant fact – that male and female genitalia are not constructed with equal facility for orgasm. In the male, orgasm corresponds with ejaculation, which has a very clear biological function. No such biological function has been demonstrated for the female orgasm despite many attempts to do so. There have been several theories about how female orgasm might facilitate conception (for example, by sucking sperm into the uterus), but the best available evidence does not lend support to them. Apparently, a woman is just as likely to get pregnant if she does not have orgasm as when she does.

Another common idea is that female orgasm has a rewarding ('reinforcement') function, causing the female to be more interested in sex or to consolidate her bond to a particular male. This sounds plausible, but evolutionary analysis indicates that it is unlikely to be true. Studies of animal behaviour in the wild, including observations of our nearest relatives like the chimpanzee, show that female orgasm seldom occurs in the normal course of events. Usually the male completes his performance by ejaculating within a matter of seconds, giving the female little chance of being aroused, let alone fulfilled. Nevertheless female monkeys do have the physiological apparatus necessary for orgasm; if they are taken into the laboratory and given protracted clitoral stimulation, they eventually achieve it (just as the most 'frigid' of women can usually be brought to orgasm with a vibrator).

Interestingly, female orgasm has occasionally been observed in captive monkeys who have more time to experiment, but usually in the context of 'lesbian' contact. Sometimes when a female monkey mounts another female she will make pelvic thrusts that culminate in muscular spasms suggestive of orgasm. However, this only happens to the monkey who is doing the mounting, not the one that is being mounted, whether by a male or a female.

If female orgasm does not occur in the wild it presumably has no selective advantage and therefore it is difficult to see how it could have evolved any separate function of its own within the human species. Surely, if it did have any biological function for the human female, it would appear with much greater frequency and reliability than it does.

The idea that women in uninhibited, 'primitive' tribes are more orgasmic than the 'repressed' European housewife (Sherfey, 1972) is also a feminist myth. Most tribal and rural women fare even worse than urban-dwelling Anglo-Americans and some, such as the Inis Beag off the coast of Ireland, have no concept of female orgasm at all. As Margaret Mead (1967) notes: 'that whole societies can ignore climax as an aspect of female sexuality must be related to a very much lesser need for such climax'.

Female orgasm as a luxury

Why does female orgasm occur at all? The best explanation so far is that of the Californian anthropologist Donald Symons (1979) who suggests that the capacity for orgasm in females stems from the fact that they share with males the basic neurological mechanisms that underlie a capacity which is biologically important only for males. For the sake of simplicity the genetic blueprints for males and females remain as similar as possible without incurring reproductive disadvantage. Thus a female canary has all the mechanisms for singing but does not demonstrate this ability unless injected with male hormone. The human male has vestigial nipples which are quite useless to him and are not erotically sensitive unless he is given oestrogen. A woman's clitoris is likewise a vestigial penis and, as such, is rather small and not located in such a place that heterosexual intercourse is the optimal method of stimulation. If sufficient clitoral stimulation is given, orgasm will occur, but a great deal of manual or oral attention may be necessary in addition to, or instead of, intercourse if the average woman is to be guaranteed the experience (see Figure 8).

Impressive confirmation of Symons's 'artefact' theory of female orgasm comes from the discovery that male hormones increase a woman's sexual responsiveness – although with the risk of masculinizing side-effects like hair on the chin (Kane, Lipton and Ewing, 1969). By contrast, attempts to treat female orgasm difficulty by using anti-anxiety drugs to counter the supposed inhibitions deriving from upbringing and religion have repeatedly failed (Wilson, 1988).

This does not devalue the female orgasm in any way or the efforts made by sex therapists and women's consciousness groups to help women achieve it. Fingers have not evolved for playing the piano, but many of us can learn to do so and give ourselves

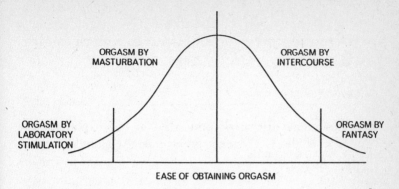

Figure 8 Normal distribution of orgasmic ability in women (from Wilson, 1988).

and other people a great deal of pleasure in the process. Likewise, many women who have not experienced orgasm can learn the skill and their male partners can be taught to assist. However, it would help enormously if we abandoned the myth that men and women are 'made for each other' – that is, constructed in such a way that in the absence of any pathology they will naturally experience simultaneous orgasm during intercourse. Orgasm is natural for men, but for women it is better understood as a skill that can be developed with appropriate training and which can provide a great deal of pleasure to both partners. A full understanding of the differing sexual response cycles of men and women, and the biological basis of this difference, is fundamental to the success of sex therapy.

The resistance of sex problems to social change was seen in the *Sun* survey described in Chapter 4. In view of the increased frankness of modern society and all the books and articles that have been written about how to improve our sex lives, we might have hoped that the younger generation (people under thirty) would have fewer sexual problems such as guilt and lack of orgasm than their parents' generation. However, comparisons based on a sample of over four thousand women (Table 5) show that these problems persist in almost exactly the same proportions

Table 5 Sexual difficulties of men and women, under and over thirty years of age

Age	Male (N = 1862)		Female (N = 2905)	
	<30	>30	<30	>30
Impotence	25	29	6	7
Too quick orgasm	59	53	12	14
Inability to have orgasm	23	23	44	41
Painful intercourse	18	13	45	37
Disgust	5	4	8	9
Guilt	15	13	19	18
Anxiety/fear	14	14	19	16
Boredom/lack of interest	21	17	35	36

Source: Wilson, 1988.

and with just the same difference between men and women (Wilson, 1988).

More than 40 per cent of women, both young and middle-aged, report difficulty in achieving orgasm, and more than half the men in both age-groups complain that their orgasm is often too quick (the reverse of retarded female orgasm). Guilt and anxiety remain as minority problems with both sexes (about 14 per cent of men and 18 per cent of women), but perhaps most striking are the numbers of women who suffer painful intercourse (around 40 per cent) or are simply bored and uninterested in sex (around 35 per cent).

Disorders of desire

The high proportion of women declaring a lack of interest in sex has resulted in a fashionable new complaint to which sex therapists have recently devoted much attention (Kaplan, 1979). A few decades ago a woman who manifested sexual inclinations like those of the average man would have been deemed pathological by psychiatrists and diagnosed as suffering from 'nymphomania'. Today the woman who shows sexual inclinations much like those of the typical woman runs the risk of being diagnosed as suffering from 'inhibited sexual desire'. It seems that the medical fraternity, like society at large, is never entirely comfortable with the range of libidos displayed by the female sex. In Victorian times women were expected to behave like ladies; today it seems they are often expected to behave like men.

The term 'inhibited sexual desire' has built into it a theoretical assumption that the women it describes have a high libido that has been suppressed by some external, social or environmental force. As with the Masters and Johnson approach to orgasm difficulty, the presumption is that unhealthy attitudes, strict upbringing, religious devoutness, learned anxiety, or some other encumbrance, is responsible for the difficulty. But an alternative possibility is that the desire was never really there in the first place.

Numerous surveys have indicated that a high proportion of women are fairly indifferent to sex for long periods of their life. Studies in which men and women are asked to rank their pleasures in order of enjoyment show repeatedly that whereas sex is the favourite for most men, many women prefer knitting, gardening and watching television. Recently I led some group discussions among ordinary British women about their attitudes towards sex. I was amazed how frequently expressions like 'My husband's very good – he doesn't bother me too often these days' cropped up. Other women would proudly describe the tactics they used to avoid sex with husbands and boyfriends – pretending to be asleep, feigning headaches, etc.

As with orgasm difficulty and premature ejaculation, lack of desire for sex appears as a major problem because average male and female arousal patterns are poorly synchronized. Typical male sexuality includes ready arousal to a wide variety of stimuli, starting from visual stimuli alone. Men may become sexually aroused just by looking at women, whereas most women need something more than this – usually the addition of olfactory and tactile cues (not to mention favourable emotional circumstances).

To the evolutionary theorist the reason is obvious. While it is advantageous for men to be easily turned on by the mere sight of a nude woman, since this serves gene proliferation, quick arousal is disadvantageous for women because it interferes with their strategy of careful mate appraisal. Inhibited sexual desire is therefore, like orgasm difficulty, better regarded as a normal rather than pathological condition.

Since lack of desire occurs as a result of a male–female discrepancy in sexual inclination, we might ask why sex therapists define it more as a female problem than male. After all, if the male partner was equally uninterested in sex there would be no problem, so it is really as much his 'fault' as hers. Perhaps the reason is that libido cannot easily be reduced except by chemical or surgical means, whereas an interest in sex can be developed by the use of erotica, fantasy, role-playing, subtle foreplay and other forms of psychological stimulation (Gillan and Gillan, 1976). Thus the female partner is more usually seen as a suitable case for treatment than the man.

There is of course one 'disorder of desire' that affects men more strikingly than women – the boredom that arises from repetitive sex with the same partner. (Recall the discussion of the 'Coolidge Effect' in Chapter 2.) The need for periodic recharging of libido by novel females that is seen in most mammals is another manifestation of the male's reproductively optimal 'promiscuity strategy'. This presents a problem, for men especially, over the course of a long marriage and is responsible for a great deal of adultery. Progressive 'contempt due to familiarity' (at least as regards sexual excitement) is an almost inevitable outcome of sexually exclusive marriage. As noted earlier, it is not unusual for sex therapists to see men who are unable to achieve erection with their wives but perfectly capable of stud-like prowess with their new secretary. Again, what is observed is not a disease but a normal biological phenomenon based on natural sex differences, and realistic solutions must therefore be sought.

Despite the recent women's movement, sex remains much less of a preoccupation, and much less rewarding as an experience, to women than to men. While it would be nice to hope that this state of affairs could be altered by a revision of sex-role attitudes, socio-biology gives little cause for optimism. The sort of problems than men and women experience in their sex lives seem to be more a part of their basic nature than the particular social climate in which they are raised. It seems inevitable that women will continue to have problems based on lack of desire, discomfort during sex and difficulty in achieving orgasm. Men will continue to have problems with being aroused by inappropriate and unacceptable stimuli (ranging from rubber garments to the neighbour's daughter) and in maintaining romantic attention and physical stimulation long enough to satisfy their legitimate partners. The belief expressed by Griffitt and Hatfield (1985) that 'the momentum of contemporary cultural change might be expected to erase (or perhaps reverse) current male–female sexual response differences in the relatively near future' is not just over-optimistic, it is totally forlorn.

6 · *Talent and Achievement*

Evolutionary theory proposes that the major basis of gender differentiation is the specialization of males as hunters and warriors, while females have become specialized as mothers and nurses. In the past this would have been read as implying group fitness (an advantage to the species), but today the concept of reproductive competition is thought more important, especially the idea that males have had to compete for access to females more vigorously than females have had to compete for male attention.

It would be surprising if such evolutionary pressure had not left its mark on the body, brain and behaviour of humans. As indicated in Table 2, we would expect males to be bigger, stronger and faster than females and to be equipped with mental skills relevant to territorial defence and weapon development. Certain temperamental traits such as aggressiveness, persistence and courage would also seem well fitted to the male specialization. Females, by contrast, would be well served by qualities of physical endurance, communicative skills, social attachment and security-seeking. All of these expected differences have been documented with more or less certainty (Seward and Seward, 1980; Ellis, 1986).

This chapter focuses on the differences in mental aptitude that may help to explain certain educational strengths and weaknesses and occupational divergences between the sexes. The way in which society manages the differences that do exist will be discussed in Chapter 8.

Origins of genius

I shall begin this discussion of sex differences in ability and achievement in the place where the most striking and controversial gender differences are observed. Virtually all of the people throughout history whose achievements are acknowledged as products of undisputed genius have one thing in common. They come from a great variety of geographical, national, social and religious backgrounds, but they are all male. Starting with names like Da Vinci, Newton, Einstein, Galton, Shakespeare, Edison, Goethe, Beethoven, Mozart, Wagner and Picasso, we might have to fill many pages before the first comparable woman would appear. When we consider the claims of women for inclusion in a list of outstanding accomplishments, their contributions can be seen mostly in the fields of literature (Jane Austen, Virginia Woolf), humanitarianism (Florence Nightingale, Mother Theresa) or politics (Margaret Thatcher, Golda Meir), rather than science, technology, music or fine art.

The supremacy of men in the field of scientific achievement can also be seen in the record of Nobel prizes awarded for physics, chemistry and medicine/physiology. Reviewing the background of the 164 recipients of these prizes between 1900 and 1950, Moulin (1955) noted that only three were women and they had all shared prizes with their husbands. The only exception was Madame Curie, who after sharing a prize with husband Pierre was later awarded another one independently. In a follow-up study by Berry (1981), the sex of the recipients was not mentioned at all. Berry describes the national origin, race, personality and social background of prize-winners, even the age at which their father died, but he does not mention whether any were female. When I contacted him for further information he explained that there were so few women in his sample he didn't think them worth mentioning. Apparently there has been no appreciable increase in the number of women receiving Nobel prizes for science in recent years.

In a recently published book on scientific genius, Simonton (1988) discusses every imaginable demographic and personality factor that might be related to scientific brilliance, including such things as age, birth order and persistence, but sex or gender do not appear in his index. Is this because the gender issue is too hot to handle, or are we supposed to assume without inquiry that genius is a purely male phenomenon? Certainly, raising this question in public today is no way to make female friends, but it is surely intellectual cowardice to side-step it in a book specifically about the topic.

Few social learning theorists or feminists, if pressed, would deny the preponderance of male genius, but would proffer an explanation in terms of the limited educational opportunities for women throughout history and general discouragement to achieve outside the realm of motherhood and the home. This explanation seems to be unsatisfactory on a number of counts.

1 Variations in the social position of women do not seem to be accompanied by any change in the sex ratio of geniuses. For example, despite the increased number of women in science laboratories in the last three or four decades, the outstanding discoveries are still mostly made by men.

2 Many male geniuses have to override considerable disadvantage in their educational or social background and considerable social or religious opposition before their contributions are recognized. Galileo, despite being old, feeble, and virtually blind, was imprisoned by the Vatican for his heretical support of the heliocentric theory. Michael Faraday was the son of an itinerant tinker, had practically no schooling and could not afford any books. Isaac Newton came from a family of small farmers, was a premature child so puny and weak that he was not expected to live and received a poor education at the local village school. Charles Dickens and Charlie Chaplin both came from backgrounds of working-class poverty that they capitalized upon in their art. Charles Darwin defied his religious training and risked social ostracism by advocating evolution theory. Richard Wagner had virtually no musical training but taught himself harmony by buying a book in his late teens. George Washington Carver emerged from a background of civil war and slavery in Missouri to become one of America's greatest biological scientists, despite constant

hunger, poverty and ill health and having been denied education because of his colour. Social and educational advantages cannot be held accountable for the achievements of men such as these, so why should disadvantage be invoked to account for the absence of female achievement?

3 Social learning theory does not adequately explain why a proportion of women do occasionally achieve quite well in certain areas (e.g. literature and politics) but not in others (e.g. science and architecture). Music composition is an interesting case in point, since it is a male-dominated profession despite the fact that girls are given more than equal encouragement to learn music at school and there are many accomplished women performers. British composer Peter Maxwell Davies recalls asking to study music at high school in Manchester and was told very firmly by the headmaster, 'This is not a girls' school!' For hundreds of years European ladies have been expected to sing and play an instrument such as the piano as a social grace, and yet the great composers have without exception been men.

In view of these objections to the 'social inhibition' hypothesis it would seem more fruitful to seek an explanation for the appearance of male genius in constitutional factors. But which factors are most relevant – intellectual, motivational or temperamental?

Mental ability

It is widely acknowledged that with respect to overall intelligence there are no obvious differences between men and women. This is partly because the most commonly used IQ tests have been purposely constructed so that male and female superiorities cancel each other out when total scores are calculated, but it remains interesting that there was no great difficulty in designing the tests in such a way. Women usually out-perform men on tests of verbal ability, the difference being most striking with young children who are just learning to talk and diminishing progressively so that it is barely detectable in adulthood. Men are better than women at dealing with mathematical and spatial problems; the difference being fairly small in childhood but becoming quite marked at adolescence (when sex hormones are reactivated). The sex difference in spatial ability may even be observed in lower mammals such as rats (Dawson, 1972).

A number of sensorimotor functions also show sex differences. Men have better daylight vision and depth perception, and faster reaction times. Women have better night vision, are more sensitive to touch and most smells (depending partly on the phase in their cycle), and have better hearing (especially in the higher ranges). They have less tolerance for loud sounds and better manual dexterity and fine co-ordination (Seward and Seward, 1980; Moir and Jessell, 1989).

Social learning theory is not often called upon to explain these sensory differences, and some of them are far from trivial. For example, it has been estimated that above sixty decibels a noise sounds about twice as loud to women as to men. This difference could well acocunt for many domestic squabbles about the ideal volume for the hi-fi or television.

Spatial intelligence

Since good spatial awareness is the best-documented gender difference in mental ability it may be useful to give some examples of its application. About twice as many women as men have difficulty in reading maps and acknowledge a tendency to confuse left and right. Quite a high proportion of women (even those who have been university educated) apparently fail to grasp the principle that the surface of a liquid remains horizontal when the container is tilted, a drawing completion task known as the Water Level Test (Figure 9). In a related test called the Rod and Frame, it has been found that when women are asked to adjust a rod to the vertical they are more influenced by a tilt on the surrounding frame than are men. This has led to the characterization of women as more 'field dependent' than men. The field dependence of women is also held reponsible for the relative difficulty they have in finding given shapes that have

Figure 9 Examples of spatial tasks on which males score reliably better than females (adapted from Halpern, 1986).

(a) *The Water Level Test*
Assume the glasses are half full of water and draw a line to indicate the top of the water. About 60 per cent of women, but very few men, tilt the water level in parallel with the glass.

(b) *The Rod and Frame Test*
Subjects have to adjust a movable rod to the vertical within a tilted rectangular frame. Men more often give the correct response (left), whereas women are influenced by the context (right).

(c) *Embedded Figures*
Find the shape on the left within the pattern on the right. Women have more difficulty in locating the hidden shape.

been hidden within a complex visual pattern (the Embedded Figures Test).

The superiority of men at tennis is often attributed to their muscular strength, yet small men like Rod Laver and John McEnroe often show supremacy over larger men, so spatial processing is more likely to be responsible for the sex difference. In any case, the strength argument rather collapses when it comes to board games like chess that also depend upon spatial ability. The top woman chess player in the world ranks only about two-thousandth in the overall league, so that adult chess tournaments generally have to be sexually segregated. Such segregation is not necessary for Scrabble competitions or quizzes such as 'Mastermind' which depend more on the retrieval of verbal information; these are just as likely to be won by women as men. (Some young girls have shown exceptional promise in mathematics and chess, usually as a result of intensive coaching by their fathers, but their performance is not generally sustained beyond puberty, for reasons to be discussed shortly.)

Although men cause an equal share of traffic accidents and are more likely to be involved in fatal crashes, they generally do so by driving too fast and aggressively and under the influence of alcohol at night. Women cause more accidents that are due to perceptual errors, distraction and misjudgement, even though they tend to drive short distances, slowly, while sober, and in broad daylight (Storie, 1977). The frequently heard claim that women must be better drivers because their insurance premiums are lower is wrong because it does not take account of the fact that men drive more often and over longer distances than women. In fact, trying to have it both ways, advocates of women drivers also claim that their lack of skill is due to inexperience. Men are more dangerous drivers, but they are also more skilled. They have more accidents due to drunkenness and recklessness and fewer due to incompetence, the result being that when male and female drivers collide they are equally likely to be responsible for the accident.

There is some evidence that spatial ability is not distributed in the population in a 'normal' bell-shaped curve with most people at middle levels but rather shows a bi-modal (on–off) tendency.

Those women who do have high-level spatial ability have much the same facility as high-level males. However, there are about twice as many men as women in the high-level ability group. This observation has led to the suggestion that spatial ability might depend upon a simple genetic mechanism, a sex-linked recessive gene located somewhere on the X chromosome, like that which is responsible for the preponderance of colour blindness in men (Buffery and Gray, 1972).

However, other evidence suggests that the Y chromosome is also involved in spatial ability. The test case is Turner's syndrome, in which the individual has only one sex chromosome, the female X (a pattern normally designated XO). If spatial ability was X-linked, these women should be equal to males with respect to spatial problem-solving. In fact women with Turner's syndrome are of normal verbal intelligence but display a specific 'space-form blindness', an inability to recall visual patterns, draw figures, use road maps, etc. – in fact an exaggerated form of the typical female disadvantage in relation to males. Clearly the lack of an X chromosome is not the equivalent of having a Y, and both X and Y chromosomes seem to be involved in determining the male superiority in spatial thinking.

Research has shown that spatial ability is influenced by sex hormones. For example, Dawson (1972) studied a group of West African males who had been feminized by a disease called kwashiokor (inability of the liver to inactivate oestrogen in the male). This condition, which results in a build-up of female hormone often to the extent of full breast development and atrophy of the testicles, may result from malnutrition, since it was also observed in European prisoners of war held by the Japanese. Men affected by this syndrome were found to be higher in verbal ability than control males, lower on spatial and mathematical ability, and more field dependent – in other words, they show a typically female pattern of abilities.

Particularly interesting in connection with the theory that homosexuality results from sex hormone effects during brain development is the finding that gay men perform more like women than heterosexual men when dealing with spatial tasks of the kind shown in Figure 9 (Sanders and Ross-Field, 1986). On the Water Level Test, for example, there was virtually no overlap between the scores of heterosexual men and women, and the scores of gay men were clearly in the range of the latter. It thus seems that the sex hormones set brain mechanisms for sex orientation and mental ability in parallel.

There is some argument as to whether it is male or female hormones that are primarily responsible for the appearance of the sex difference in spatial ability. Until recently it was assumed that the male hormone testosterone somehow led to an enhancement of spatial ability in men. However, the Danish psychologist Nyborg (1981) has reported that this sex difference, which is sharpened soon after adolescence, results from a decrease in female spatial ability rather than an increase in the male ability. Therefore an inhibitory effect of the female hormone oestrogen seems to be to blame. In support of this, he notes variations in spatial ability occurring within women at different points in their monthly cycle, the lowest spatial performance appearing during times of maximum oestrogen secretion. Nevertheless, the effect of oestrogen is by no means simple and straightforward. Nyborg and his colleagues believe that the total evidence suggests a curvilinear relationship between oestrogen and spatial ability, with both very low and very high levels being detrimental to spatial performance.

Whatever the genetic and hormonal basis of male spatial intelligence, it seems to be partly mediated by a greater degree of specialization of the right cerebral hemisphere. Studies of the effects of localized brain lesions and the behaviour of split-brain animals (animals operated upon so that the left and right sides of their brain function separately) confirm that in both sexes the left hemisphere usually controls speech while the right hemisphere is more concerned with the spatial relations. However, this hemispheric specialization seems to be more marked in the male brain, particularly in the sense that the right hemisphere is reserved more exclusively for spatial thinking (Harris, 1978). This reduces the safety factor implied by having a duplicate 'back-up' brain should the left hemisphere get into difficulty (dyslexia and stammering, for example, are more common in males), but the gain is perhaps seen in extraordinary spatial conceptions like Copernicus's heliocentric theory of the solar system, Einstein's theory of relativity and Beethoven's Ninth Symphony.

Differing thought processes

The intelligence and aptitude tests commonly used in educational and industrial selection may actually underestimate the divergence between male and female thinking patterns because they deal only with outcome (final test scores) and not with process (the manner in which they are achieved).

In a fascinating study by Max Coltheart and colleagues of the University of London (Coltheart, Hull and Slater, 1975), male and female students were asked to work through the alphabet twice. On the first occasion their task was to count the letters which had curves in their shape (BCDGJ, etc.) and the second time through they had to count letters that are sounded with an 'ee' (BCDEG, etc.). Men are markedly superior on the first (visual) task, while women were clearly better on the second (phonetic) task. A number of experiments in this idiom indicate that women often apply verbal techniques to solve mathematical and spatial problems, while men bring spatial skills to bear on linguistic problems. In each case some degree of speed and efficiency is usually lost, which may partly account for the differences between men and women that appear in the test scores.

Some studies of sex differences in mathematical performance show that girls are superior to boys at young ages but are overtaken and eventually left behind at more advanced levels of education. The reason seems to be that girls are particularly good at consolidating automatic rules for computation. This manifests itself as good early performance, but they lack the flexibility to attack problems from different directions, which becomes progressively important at higher levels of mathematical performance (Marshall and Smith, 1987). This could be because verbal instructions are used by girls to store arithmetical rules, whereas boys approach problems in a more visual/spatial way. Alternatively, personality traits such as conformity (in girls) versus independence (in boys) could have something to do with the difference. The obedience to rules displayed by girls in most aspects of life may inhibit originality in higher mathematics and science, while the male tendency towards general delinquency may facilitate lateral thinking.

Does ability account for genius?

Can these intellectual specialities explain the particular cultural achievements of men and women? It does seem that the areas in which men excel, like physics, astronomy, chess and music, depend more on spatial and mathematical skills than on verbal skills. Likewise, the areas in which women have competed successfully with men over the centuries, like novel-writing and politics, depend more on linguistic ability (as well as intuition and empathy). This is consistent with the possibility that biologically based intellectual predispositions are at least partly responsible for the appearance of genius.

The main argument against this idea is that these differences between men and women in verbal and spatial ability are on average fairly small and there is a great deal of overlap between them (Hyde, 1981). Some critics of the biological viewpoint argue that such small differences in intellectual aptitudes (seldom accounting for more than 15 per cent of the variance) could not by themselves be responsible for the overwhelming preponderance of male genius in the history of the world. Surely social encouragement and expectations must add considerable power to any natural advantage men might have?

The answer is: not necessarily. When considering genius we are dealing with something exceptional, so the abilities of average people have little relevance. There is considerable overlap between men and women in their ability to play tennis, yet no woman would appear in a list of the world's top thousand tennis players. Chris Evert admitted that even as world champion she could hardly take one game per set off her husband John Lloyd.

As we have noted, a similar state of affairs prevails with respect to chess-playing. A small average difference becomes very significant at the extreme ends of the distribution, because even with overlapping curves the top few per cent nearly all lie within one group. And if more than one attribute is relevant to genius, as seems likely, the sex ratio may be radically tilted.

Geniuses as freaks

We may even be dealing with 'freak' individuals rather than extremes of the normal distribution, just as some forms of mental retardation are qualitatively different from other forms of low intelligence. Childhood autism is of particular interest in this regard. This is a biologically based lack of interest in (or even aversion to) verbal and social communication, and it is much more common in boys than girls. Occasionally, autistic children are found to have exceptionally high mathematical, spatial or musical abilities, which baffle parents and teachers in that they emerge quite spontaneously without any special instruction or incentive (Rimland, 1964). The fact that such precocious children do not often go on to make their mark in society does not diminish the likelihood that they are in some way akin to the freak, highly specialized mentality that predisposes to genius, and it is interesting that 'idiot-savants', as they are sometimes called, display their unique talents in characteristically right-hemisphere, male-type skills.

Similarly, more males than females are diagnosed as manic and schizophrenic (at least until the menopause, when the production of female hormones is sharply reduced), and there is a good deal of research suggesting a link between these psychoses and creativity. While I would not suggest that all psychotics are unrecognized geniuses, men like Darwin, Einstein, Picasso and Beethoven might easily be dismissed as madmen in some cultural climates, and there are many creative geniuses who have teetered on the brink of clinical psychosis – for instance, Helmholtz, Tesla, Van Gogh and Gerard Manley Hopkins.

It appears that all kinds of brain abnormalities, or ex-

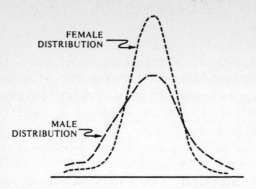

Figure 10   The distributions of male and female IQs (adapted from Lehrke, 1978).

ceptionality, are more common in men than women. One result of this is to spread the range of IQs in men relative to women (Figure 10). In other words, there are more men at the bright and dull ends of the spectrum. This apparently occurs because the second X chromosome in women has an averaging effect, cancelling out extreme tendencies based on the other (Lehrke, 1978). Just as very low IQ scores represent mental handicap, the very high scores might provide the pool from which geniuses emerge (after all, the other influences have also made their mark).

Perhaps male superiority in mathematical and spatial reasoning, combined with the appearance of 'freak' high levels of intelligence, might be sufficient to explain the preponderance of male genius, but we still have other strong candidates to consider.

Temperamental factors

Another possible source of the preponderance of male achievement in the world is constitutional personality and motivation. Men tend to be more assertive, ambitious and grandiose in their schemes than women, and more single-minded in seeking recognition and greatness. Aggressiveness and dominance are characteristic of males in all human societies and nearly all animal species (with rare exceptions like the hamster) and these traits have also been traced to the effects of testosterone (Goldberg, 1977). It is therefore no surprise to find that women who do compete with men in traditionally male occupations (e.g. lawyers and managers) show signs of having been exposed to more male hormones than women in more typically feminine roles such as nurse, secretary and housewife (Purifoy and Koopmans, 1979; Schindler, 1979, Wilson, 1983).

From conception to completion, Wagner's Ring Cycle took thirty-four years to compose, a remarkable example of persistence and determination. Many women have written successful songs, among them some very popular Victorian ballads, but they have seldom put together musical works on a grander scale such as operas, symphonies or even musical comedies. It is difficult to escape the conclusion that some factor such as intrinsic motivation or 'scale of thinking' is another contributor to artistic genius. A willingness to take risks in order to satisfy curiosity and break new ground, as exemplified by mountain-climbing and space travel, is also typical of the male temperament and may account for many major scientific discoveries and original departures within the arts.

Persistence in tackling problems might seem like the kind of characteristic that could be increased by social expectations, but experimental evidence suggests that this is really only true for females. A representative study is that made by Susan Harter (1975), who worked with eleven-year-old boys and girls. The task involved learning a sequence of colour buttons to push in order to release a marble on each trial. There were two patterns, one reasonably easy to learn and the other impossible. The main issue was how long boys and girls would persist in trying to solve the impossible problem. Half the subjects in each gender group were tested with an experimenter present and making encouraging remarks; the other half were studied working alone. Results showed that boys generally persisted longer at the insoluble task than girls and that the presence of the experimenter increased the persistence of the girls, whereas the boys worked longer when they were alone. This is consistent with a great deal of other evidence that boys are primarily motivated by a need to achieve 'mastery', while girls are more oriented towards the goal of social approval. Putting it another way, social support may enhance female achievement, but male ambition seems to be fairly intrinsic.

Although some might argue that these differences develop as a result of social learning experiences, it seems more than coincidental that they take the exact form that would be predicted by evolutionary theory. Parallel differences can also be observed in other animals, and in very early infancy, before a child even knows whether it is male or female. For example, if one-year-old babies are separated from their mothers and toys by a fence-like barrier, girls tend to stay in the middle and cry for assistance, while boys spend more time at the ends apparently trying to find a way around it (Goldberg and Lewis, 1969). Also, as noted in Chapter 2, male and female hormones given to a mother in late pregnancy have power to influence the degree of dependency of the child, male hormones pushing the child towards greater self-sufficiency, and female hormones causing a greater degree of dependence. Evolutionary theory is consistent with all the evidence; social learning has nothing to say about most of it.

Sporting prowess

The determination factor is probably another reason men excel at most sports, including those in which size and strength do not seem important. Top women players in sports such as bowls, darts and snooker report that men concentrate harder and use more aggressive, risk-taking tactics in their play; women are more easily distracted and play for safety rather than victory. Champion darts player Maureen Flowers said in a *Sunday Times* interview (1982): 'It seems harder for a woman to concentrate; she gets distracted. Men can shut everything out. They take it much more seriously. They're more ambitious.' Similarly, the women's world champion snooker player Vera Selby doubted that women would ever equal the top men. 'I have come to the conclusion that the women will never be as good as the men. In certain things women do apply themselves better. But it seems that men apply themselves more thoroughly to sport. They've got much more enthusiasm and aggression.' Spatial ability may be important in games such as these, but the competitive spirit, the will to win, probably accentuates the gender gap.

The biological basis of male dominance, aggressiveness, independence, determination and achievement motivation seems to be fairly well established, and these temperamental factors seem likely to be responsible to some degree for male creativity and achievement. These personality factors, taken together with the special cognitive skills of men, would seem to have sufficient power to account for the observed preponderance of male genius. Obviously the case is not closed. Given sufficient social encouragement we may see more women making outstanding contributions to science and art. There is little evidence of this happening so far, but the next hundred years or so may be illuminating.

Creativity as courtship display

Finally, there is one other way of looking at male creativity and productivity that may also shed some light. In order to gain access to females, the males of most species have to provide some kind of performance or display; their size alone may not be sufficient. Often these displays are carried on the body of the male, like the peacock's colourful tail, the antlers of a buck and possibly the beard of a man. In other species, however, the display depends upon some form of creative effort. The outstanding example is the New Guinea bower-bird, which attracts females by building an elaborate construction assembled out of any brightly coloured objects that it can find or pilfer. The more impressive his bower, the better his chances of attracting female partners.

Although this species is fairly unusual, and the courtship rituals of most mammals are less impressive (the chimpanzee merely leaps up and down or waves a branch he has broken off a tree), it is nevertheless a rule of nature that males must demonstrate worthiness in some way to gain mating privileges. Building the Taj Mahal, or Disneyland, painting pictures, composing symphonies and operas, and making Nobel-prize-winning contributions to science – all, ultimately, may be motivated by a need to impress women.

Conclusion

It is widely accepted that physical gender differences have developed as a result of specialization of function and repro-ductive competition, and there is every reason to suppose that mental and emotional differences have evolved in parallel. If it is advantageous for males to be good hunters and fighters, in order to feed and protect their family and succeed in competition for access to females, then they will tend to be faster, stronger, bolder, more exploratory and equipped with spatial skills for geographical mobility and weapon construction. If it is advantageous to females to nurse offspring, prepare them for adult life and promote family groupings, then they will tend to have a greater capacity for physical endurance, nurturance and attachment, a preference for security, and social and com-municative skills. All these differences have been observed throughout history.

In case anyone should imagine that these ideas are original, I should note that they are quite explicit in the writings of Charles Darwin more than a hundred years ago. Darwin observed that men have to use their brains not just to stay alive but also to compete for women, and this has led to greater persistence, cunning and resourcefulness, as well as superior physical strength, in the human male.

Amongst the half-human progenitors of man, and amongst savages, there have been struggles between the males during many generations for the possession of females. But mere bodily strength would do little for victory, unless associated with courage, perseverance, and determined energy. With social animals, the young males have to pass through many a contest before they win a female, and the older males have to retain their females by renewed battles. . . . To avoid enemies or to attack them with success, to capture wild animals, and to fashion weapons, requires the aid of higher mental faculties, namely observation, reason, invention, or imagination. . . . Consequently . . . we would expect that they would tend to be transmitted chiefly to the male offspring. . . . Thus man has ultimately become superior to women. It is indeed fortunate that the law of equal transmission of characters to both sexes prevails with mammals; otherwise it is probable that man would have become as superior in mental endowment to women, as the peacock is in ornamental plumage to the peahen. (Darwin, 1871, p. 564)

Thus Darwin clearly attributes the ingenuity and perseverance of man to an evolutionary history of inter-male competition. As regards the positive qualities of women, Darwin maintains that they are more kind-hearted and self-sacrificing because of their maternal instincts and that these attributes carry over to the way they treat other adults. He also acknowledges women's superior powers of intuition, rapid perception and imitation, though he dismisses these as somewhat primitive attributes.

As a working example of how ingenuity may pay off in the inter-male dominance struggle, it is worth describing an incident that occurred in a troup of chimpanzees observed by Jane Goodall (1971). One day she saw a subordinate male pick up a pair of empty kerosene cans from near her camp and carry them up to the top of a hill; below a group of dominant males were eating some bananas that she had laid out as bait. The chimpanzee then proceeded to run down the hill towards the dominant males, banging the two cans together to create an awful din. Startled by the clamour, the dominant males rushed off for cover, deserting their bananas. The result of this episode was that the subordinate male not only got the bananas but was elevated to the rank of alpha male with all its attendant sexual (and breeding) privileges. This illustrates the principle that intellectual prowess may supplant physical strength as a means to achieving dominance in the animal hierarchy, thus helping to account for the startling evolution of human brain power.

Since surveys that ask men and women what they seek in a partner repeatedly find that men look for physical attractiveness while women put a higher value on intelligence, it is reasonable to conclude that women are at the cutting edge of the selective pressure that gave rise to our formidable brains (Gallup, 1986).

It is not up to me to make recommendations for social policy on the basis of such a theory. This is the point where science gives way to politics. Suffice it to say that I fully favour equality of opportunity in the sense of evaluating all candidates for academic and professional positions as individuals, rather than representatives of a gender group. Since there is considerable overlap between men and women in all areas of ability, there is no justification, moral or scientific, for doing otherwise. By the same token there is little justification for the programmes of reverse discrimination that have sprung up both in Britain and the United States to increase the proportion of women in certain specialized occupations, or political interventions aimed at overriding sex roles (e.g. by censorship of school books). Men and women are different in nature, and educational policy-makers should not indulge in fantasies to the contrary. Crude attempts to replace the old straitjacket of gender stereotypes with a new one of psychological identity are likely to be hurtful as well as fruitless.

7 · *Aggression and Crime*

The previous chapter dealt with an area in which men appear as 'superior' to women – that of spatial intelligence and artistic and scientific creativity. In case it should seem that I am just breast-beating on behalf of my own gender, let us consider a field in which men emerge with less credit. It is a well-known fact that men are more aggressive than women, more prone to psycho-pathic personality disorders and more inclined towards most forms of criminal misconduct.

Although some people have supposed that the criminality gap would close as women become more liberated and financially independent, there is very little evidence that this is happening (Sarri, 1979). Female crime statistics have increased slightly faster than those for men over the last decade or so, but roughly 85 per cent of all crimes are still committed by males (a ratio of more than five to one). Only for prostitution, and some-times shop-lifting, do female figures exceed those of males. Other crimes, including rape, robbery, burglary, football hooliganism and car theft, are almost exclusively male, and the indications are that they will remain so into the foreseeable future.

It is sometimes argued that arrest statistics are misleading, because the police and courts are more lenient with women offenders, and male criminals often protect their female partners. However, research does not support this 'chivalry' theory of male crime prevalence. Reviewing a wide variety of evidence, Leonard (1982) concludes that in some circumstances women receive even harsher treatment by the legal authorities than men and that 'the discrepancy between male and female crime rates is generally accurate'. This being the case, let us look at the probable reasons.

Male aggressiveness

The tendency for men to be more aggressive than women is often given as an explanation of male criminality, and there is no doubt some truth in this theory. However, this idea needs closer inspection. In a comprehensive review of all studies in which male and female subjects were compared for signs of aggression, Frodi, Macaulay and Thorne (1977) concluded that while men come out as more aggressive in most situations, there are some circumstances in which women appear just as aggressive as men. In particular, women show an equal or greater amount of aggression when such a reaction is perceived as justified or pro-social. For example, a mother will beat her children just as severely as the father, if she is able to interpret the act as being 'for their own good', and in simulated jury studies women assign sentences to hypothetical offenders that are just as punitive as those assigned by men. Margaret Thatcher's uncompromising stand on terrorism and her endorsement of the death penalty may also illustrate this point. Women are capable of being very tough where matters of principle and justice are concerned.

Ethologists (scientists who study instincts) distinguish *offensive* aggression, which is concerned with improving one's status in relation to other members of the species (i.e. competing with others for dominance), from *defensive* aggression, which is protective of oneself and one's family (especially offspring). It is only the former type of aggression that is markedly affected by male sex hormones and therefore more typical of males than females (Ellis, 1986). Females are just as capable of defensive aggression, and possibly even more so.

In studies across many different species and cultures it has been found that males engage in more 'rough-and-tumble play' (a pre-adolescent form of rank-related aggression), although the differences are most striking in primates. That this is due to male sex hormones is suggested by the fact that perinatal androgen

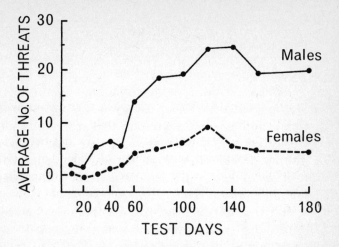

Figure 11 The natural appearance of male aggression in young Rhesus monkeys raised with surrogate (inanimate) mothers (from Harlow, 1965).

increases the tendency to play fighting in females (Quadagno, Briscoe and Quadagno, 1977). Harlow's studies of infant monkeys reared by surrogate mothers in isolation from other members of their species also confirm the innate basis of rank-related aggression (Figure 11).

Other studies have compared violent males (e.g. aggressive criminals) with non-violent males and found slightly higher levels of androgen in the blood and saliva of the violent types (e.g. Dabbs *et al.*, 1987). Interestingly, androgen variations have the same significance within groups of women prisoners. Dabbs and colleagues (1988) found higher levels of male hormone in women convicted of unprovoked violence compared with women whose violence was defensive or reactive (e.g. abused wives who killed their husbands). They also found that amount of male hormone was related to the number of prior charges in a woman's record and parole board decisions about how long they should remain in prison. Thus there is evidence that androgens are related to violent, competitive tendencies within each sex, which rather increases our confidence that the differences *between* the sexes are attributable to the same cause.

One qualification is necessary, however. While we may 'conclude beyond any doubt that androgens can alter the mammalian nervous system in a way that increases the probability of offensive aggression, thus substantially accounting for why males in all but a few rodent species display more status-related aggression then females' (Ellis, 1986), much of the important effect of male hormones has taken place before birth, let alone puberty. Castration studies demonstrate that male brains are pre-set during development in such a way that only a tiny amount of androgen is needed to activate status-related aggression in adulthood (Hart, 1974). Measures of circulating hormone may therefore be diagnostic only because they reflect the levels of androgen that prevailed during pre-natal development when brain structures were being established as male or female (see Chapter 6).

The observation that males exceed females only with respect to offensive aggression is exactly what would have been predicted from socio-biological theory. Offensive aggression is primarily concerned with jostling for rank within the (primarily male) dominance hierarchy, with maintaining and expanding territorial claims, and vying for access to females. All such competitive warmongering could be advantageous to the individual male so disposed, because it would promote the proliferation of his genes in relation to those of more peaceful, submissive and timid males. This is not to say that 'might is right' in any moral, civilized sense, but that its evolution within males may be inevitable – at least up to the point where aggression becomes so reckless that the individual runs a very high risk of getting himself killed before he has had much chance to breed.

This sort of fighting among women makes much less sense as an evolutionary strategy because there is seldom a shortage of males available for fertilization services and therefore little need to fight over them. Women might develop subtle strategies for competing for the 'bread-winning' support and protection of particular, powerful males, but their outright physical aggression is mainly reserved for direct threats to their genes, such as attacks on their body or their children. Hence women's aggression is much more typically defensive or reactive in nature. Threaten an animal's offspring and the mother will be just as ferocious as the father, if not more so.

Males, then, are not always more aggressive than females, but they usually are in situations that imply struggles for rank, territory and females. And because the opportunities for offensive aggression are much more common than situations calling for defensive fighting, aggression is much nearer the surface, and dearer to the heart, in men than women.

Aggression and anger

Another distinction between offensive and defensive aggression that may help to clarify the difference is that the latter is much more obviously connected with feelings of anger and fear. Although it is commonly supposed that all aggression is due to anger, this is by no means the case. The armed robber who holds up a security van or the politician who scores devastating points off a rival in a television debate are acting aggressively, but they do not necessarily feel anger towards the people they are trying to intimidate. Likewise, the psychopath who brought down an entire jumbo jet full of people with a bomb in his wife's suitcase probably felt no emotion at all for any of the passengers killed – he just wanted to collect the insurance he had taken out on his wife shortly beforehand.

Defensive aggression, however, is related to strong emotions, notably fear and anger. If someone attacks us or our child, or if we catch our mate *in flagrante* with another lover, we will feel fear, anger or some mixture of the two and our aggressive outburst will be the natural consummation of those strong feelings. The violent crimes that are occasionally committed by women are more likely to fall into this category, whereas men's violence frequently appears gratuitous.

This difference is quite striking with respect to the most violent crime of all – murder. The victims of male murderers can be shop assistants, police and security men, business rivals, members of rival gangs, debtors, young women, children in a school playground, in fact almost anybody. Female murderers, on the other hand, nearly always kill members of their own family or close friends.

A study of female homicide in America found that 53 per cent of the victims were husbands or lovers, 19 per cent were their own children and 16 per cent were female friends and relatives (Boudouris, 1971). Often there was evidence that the husband or lover had physically abused the woman, who then killed out of self-defence or retaliation. A high proportion of the women murderers were easily arrested, because they confessed immediately or stayed at the scene of the crime. All this is far removed from the sort of murders perpetrated by Al Capone and his mob in Chicago, Jack the Ripper in Whitechapel, or Charles Whitman, who shot thirty-eight people for target practice from a tower at Texas University.

Other effects of testosterone

It is perhaps important to remind the reader that aggression is not the only effect of the male hormone testosterone. We have already mentioned the relationship of this hormone to libido and spatial ability. Researchers have also detected its influence on dominance, persistence, energy expenditure, sensation-seeking, intolerance of frustration, and positive feelings (Dabbs *et al.*, 1988). It should also be noted that not only does testosterone affect behaviour, but levels of this hormone are in turn influenced by experience. Men who win fights and sporting contests demonstrate an increase in testosterone, while those who lose show a decrease (Elias, 1981; Mazur and Lamb, 1980; Rose, Bernstein and Gordon, 1975). It is as though the victor in an inter-male fight is being prepared for sexual reward. Thus there is a reciprocal relationship between male hormones and male behaviour, each having power to increase the other.

We have observed that testosterone levels in women have been found to be associated with competitive, traditionally male choices of occupation (see Chapter 6) and predatory, libidinous, and lesbian forms of sexual behaviour (Chapter 5). Testosterone values have also been found to be elevated in transsexual women – women who identify themselves as male in gender (Sipova and Starka, 1977). Male sex hormones are therefore present in small but variable amounts in women and, even if they do not immediately render them more or less manlike in psychological characteristics, they reflect masculinization processes that occurred during embryonic development of the brain.

Therefore it seems that male hormones are connected with a wide variety of 'macho' behaviour patterns, offensive aggression being just one of them. Psychopathy and criminal violence are extreme and anti-social forms of tendencies that are more positively manifested as assertiveness and determination. To put it another way, aggressiveness may sometimes be useful and appropriate, for example, in driving a businessman to reach the top, but it may also appear as the social problem that we call crime.

The 'supermale' syndrome

Further evidence of a genetic relationship between masculinity and crime comes from the discovery of a chromosome aberration popularly called the 'supermale' syndrome. About one man in every thousand carries an extra Y chromosome, making a total of forty-seven instead of the usual forty-six. These men with the XYY combination are not necessarily abnormal and in fact may live their lives undetected. However, it has been found that there is an increased likelihood that they will be very tall and they are about twenty times as likely as normal men to end up in the security wing of a mental hospital.

While it is not clear whether hyper-aggressiveness is responsible for this trouble (it could be some other factor such as mental defectiveness or impulsiveness), it is nevertheless interesting than an extra male chromosome produces effects that look like an anti-social extension of a masculine characteristic.

Androgenic steroids

At the Seoul Olympics a great deal of publicity was given to the use of steroids by certain athletes to enhance their performance, at least one world record being achieved by this means. These drugs – which are of course illegal – are really artificial male hormones which build stronger muscles (again, an exaggeration of the way in which men typically differ from women). Before all this publicity, and the subsequent crack-down on drugs in sport, it was estimated that about 20 per cent of boxers, weight-lifters and other athletes (both male and female) may have been using steroids to boost their performance (*The Times*, 9 December 1988).

These hormones not only increase muscle-power; they have various other side-effects which are more or less unpleasant. They increase the competitive, aggressive drive, which probably also enhances athletic performance, but they may also cause acne, headaches, liver damage, aggressive outbursts and paranoid delusions. Legal history was made in Britain in 1988 when a man was acquitted of brutally murdering his girlfriend during a violent rage that the judge accepted was caused by a steroid he was taking legitimately under medical supervision. Hence, according to the law, we may be unable to resist the demands of our hormones.

In women, androgenic steroids may cause masculinization of personality, voice and genitals as well as increases in energy and libido. In men, paradoxically, the genitals are likely to atrophy because the body's own supply of androgens is cut off to compensate for those introduced from the outside, and this may ultimately lead to breast development and infertility.

The female cycle

If hormonal balance affects our predisposition to crime, then it is reasonable to suppose that women might become more crime-prone at certain points in their monthly cycle. Indeed there is clear evidence that women are more likely to commit crimes during the pre-menstrual phase. Roughly half of all female crime, mental hospital admissions and suicide attempts occur in the week before menstruation, and four-fifths of all female crime occurs either during menstruation or the week before. Surveys have also shown higher levels of aggressiveness and impulsiveness in the pre-menstrual phase (D'Orban and Dalton, 1980; Howard, Gifford and Lumsden, 1988). Pre-menstrual tension (PMT) has been used successfully as a defence against charges of murder in several European courts, and treatment with the hormone progesterone is believed to ameliorate its worst ravages in susceptible women.

The PMT defence against violent crime in women raises interesting legal questions. Even at the most dangerous phase of her cycle a woman is still statistically less dangerous than the average man. Yet nobody would seriously argue that normal male hormones could be used as a justification for violent crime (the steroid defence is dubious enough). Feminists are also rightly concerned that court rulings in favour of PMT sufferers imply that women are unsuitable for certain important jobs, such as politician and airline pilot, because they may become emotionally unstable at certain times of the month.

The problem is that hormones certainly have the power to influence behaviour, but they seldom have total control. It is thus inappropriate and possibly even dangerous to relieve people of legal responsibility for their behaviour, as though their hormones are some alien force outside of themselves. Likewise, it is unfair to assume in advance that their hormones will render them unfit for particular occupational niches.

Female crime

Although most crime is committed by men, it is interesting to look at the types of crime that women commit with some degree of frequency, since these reveal much about the basic differences between the sexes.

Prostitution is a typically female offence and for obvious reasons. Men cannot successfully offer their bodies for sale, except occasionally to older men. This, as we have seen, is because the law of supply and demand in sex is organized so that men demand sex and women supply, on condition (i.e. in return for some favour). Prostitutes and strippers usually justify their trade on the grounds that all women are prostitutes – it is just that the length of the contract varies, from one hour for straight payment, through an evening for a meal, to marriage for a lifetime. Socio-biology implies that there is some truth in this view, however unflattering it sounds when expressed in such crude terms. What is certain is that there would be many more convictions for male prostitution if the market was there.

Other common female offences, such as using drugs and minor fraud and driving infringements, are not truly criminal in the same way as robbery and rape. They are relatively victimless crimes, with minimal violence; the sort of activities that many normal people could become involved with under certain circumstances. That is, they do not necessarily indicate an aggressive, psychopathic, 'criminal' personality.

Perhaps the only violent crime in which females are involved to any extent is terrorism. Terrorist factions frequently include a woman member, and victims and hostages report that they are often just as ferocious and cruel as the men. Notorious female terrorists that come to mind are Ulrike Meinhof of the German Red Army Faction, Leila Khaled, the Palestinian hijacker, Dr Rose Dugdale of the IRA, Joelle Aubron, who murdered the Renault chief in France, and Patty Hearst of the Symbionese Liberation Front.

If women tend to lack aggression, how do we explain the phenomenon of female terrorists? The answer may lie in the distinction made earlier between offensive and defensive aggression. Women become dangerous when they believe that they are defending their kin and that their violence is socially justified. It is this commitment to a cause that distinguishes the violent female. Men may be violent by nature; women usually need a reason – even if that reason is only acceptable to themselves. Terrorists do not usually think of themselves as criminals at all, but as passionate defenders of 'the faith'; this is why women are often numbered among them. Even the

Manson women who so brutally murdered pregnant Sharon Tate in the Hollywood Hills believed they were doing their social duty by striking against 'capitalist pigs' on behalf of their deranged guru.

This example, incidentally, highlights another circumstance in which women may find themselves involved in crime – when they are in love with a man who turns out to be a criminal. As in the case of Bonnie and Clyde, a woman may be so devoted to her lover that she follows him to inevitable destruction. In fact, women often seem to be irresistibly drawn to psychopathic males because of their hypermasculinity. Serial murderer Ted Bundy, for example, who murdered up to a hundred young women around the state of Washington, received numerous proposals of marriage from women around America while awaiting execution.

Next, let us note three other crimes that are sometimes committed by women, because they connect with characteristically female instincts rather than rank-related aggression.

First, there is shop-lifting. A simple-minded view is that women are frequently charged with this offence because they do more shopping than men. But there is a compulsive quality about the shop-lifting of some women which suggests an instinctual basis (rather equivalent to male fetishisms like stealing women's underwear). Some middle-aged and otherwise respectable women have been known to amass vast stores of food or clothing that they do not need from repeated shop-lifting excursions, and this behaviour appears to be driven more by an acquisitive, 'nest-building' instinct than by economic or aggressive motives. Some deep insecurity compels them to 'put things away for a rainy day', even though they may be aware that this behaviour is irrational and feel very guilty about it. A clue to this motivation is the fact that, while male shop-lifters are usually young delinquents, many women only begin to offend when they are elderly and their impulse control is reduced by senile brain deterioration.

Other crimes for which women are sometimes charged are child-beating and infanticide, which certainly seem like aggression, but not the same kind of aggression as that which pushes men into dominance struggles. After all, the dominance of a mother over a young child may be taken for granted; she does not need to thrash or kill her infant to prove it. Rather, these types of abuse by a mother against her own child seem more like the behaviour of an non-human mother towards the runt among her litter. It therefore seems to relate to a particular 'maternal' instinct, the elimination of deformed or otherwise unwanted offspring seen in many non-human species. Evidence for this idea comes from the fact that children murdered by their natural mothers are usually less then one year old (Daly and Wilson, 1987); older children are seldom murdered by their own parents.

Finally, there is the 'wrath of woman scorned' towards an ex-lover that gained much attention recently in connection with the films *Fatal Attraction* and *Dance with a Stranger*. Pathological jealousy, with violent and murderous consequences, does occur in men, but their rage is more often directed towards a male rival. Some women whose love has been lost or rejected become obsessionally vengeful towards the ex-lover and may end up murdering him. The original affair may be imaginary, in which case the obsessional jealousy is called De Clerembault's syndrome after the French doctor who first described it. Disorders of this kind are more common in women than men and probably derive from the intimate bonding instinct that is more characteristically female than male (Ellis, 1986). Since women are given to sacrificing more for the man they love than vice versa, they are consequently likely to be the more resentful and vindictive when he proves unworthy or unfaithful.

Male gangs

We now turn to some forms of crime and anti-social behaviour that are typically male. One is the tendency for young men to form themselves into gangs that terrorize neighbourhoods by territory-marking (for instance, scrawling graffiti on walls) and seeking confrontation with rival gangs.

This kind of behaviour, typified by the 'rumbles' between Jets and Sharks in *West Side Story*, Los Angeles drug gangs and the violence of certain football fans in European countries, has been recognized throughout history as a typically male phenomenon (Tiger, 1969). Attempts to control the vandalism and fighting that so frequently follow football matches are often ineffective because they fail to appreciate a central point – that these young men actually enjoy and seek out violence. Work on a production line, or, worse still, unemployment, is excruciatingly boring; gang warfare puts excitement back into life. The fighting that occurs is therefore not viewed by the participants as an unfortunate, accidental event but as something more like a hobby.

When a gang of male youths meets another of similar strength, there is a great deal of posturing and threatening, but they usually treat each with a degree of respect and there may be no bloodshed at all. However, if a gang encounters a lone outsider or a small helpless group outside of their own territory, they are likely to launch a vicious, cowardly attack. This is seen in such behaviour as 'queer-bashing', 'Paki-bashing' and gang rape.

Such behaviour is also seen in non-human primates such as orang-utans and chimpanzees. Jane Goodall's research group in Africa observed gangs of male chimpanzees who would patrol the borders of their territory and sadistically execute any lone intruder that they came across, some holding him down and others mercilessly beating him. One tribe of fifteen chimpanzees was seen to wipe out a smaller tribe over a period of a month simply by killing off one male at a time (Berry, 1983).

It is easy to see from this example how a tribal or gang-forming instinct would evolve among males. Males operating as a group are much more dangerous than lone rangers and have better chances of survival in the inevitable battles for supremacy among males. This instinct for gang warfare is clearly at the root of certain categories of male-dominated crime.

War

War between nations is probably an extension of the same instinct for fighting in gangs. Although not usually thought of as a criminal activity (because national ambitions are involved), war is a form of aggression in which males are at the forefront. Women are often expected to contribute to the war effort by providing back-up services such as nursing, food and munitions production, but they are seldom expected to fight on the front line. Not even the Israeli army requires that.

The basic instinct underlying war is territorial struggle, and it is clear that armies that can unite under broad banners will have the edge over smaller gangs and tribes. Hence we fight for 'king and country', 'the Emperor', 'Mother Russia' or 'Uncle Sam'. It has even been suggested that the concept of 'God' evolved as a means of uniting larger armies – groups who fight for mere kings being no match for those who fight for God. Hence the well-known historical phenomenon of 'holy wars' (Fremlin, 1974).

Rape

Finally, we come to a crime that is almost exclusively male and which particularly arouses the anger of feminists. It is frequently asserted that men do not understand the full horror of the experience of being raped and that judges are often lenient, even sympathetic, with rapists.

Paradoxically this state of affairs is exacerbated by the feminist argument that female sexuality is the same as that of males. Any man who truly believed that would be unsympathetic towards a woman who had been raped, because the chances are that he would regard the idea of being raped by women as a positive fantasy.

Some years ago, a young Mormon man was held captive by his attractive ex-girlfriend who had pursued him from the United States to Britain, where he was engaged in missionary work, and he was forced to engage in sexual activity with her. When he laid a complaint of rape against her, the media and courts reacted more with amusement than horror, most men in the street taking the attitude 'I should be so lucky'. Clearly there is widespread social consciousness of the fact that female-on-male rape is a rarity, not because men are stronger than women but because they are seldom unwilling to participate in sex, whether with partners known to them or complete strangers.

There is a popular feminist theory that rape has little to do with sex at all and is motivated by hatred of women and the desire to dominate and humiliate them (Brownmiller, 1975). This theory has difficulty in explaining why rapists choose poor, young women as victims rather than powerful, older women and why rapists themselves derive from particular age and social groups. It is also incorrect to assume that rape reflects personal or social pathology. Rape occurs in all societies, modern and primitive, as well as non-human primates such as orang-utans (see Chapter 3), and most rapists are not psychotic or otherwise mentally disordered (Petty and Dawson, 1989).

A theory of rape that fits the known facts much more comfortably is the evolutionary or socio-biological one. Thornhill and Thornhill (1987) introduce this theory by describing the sexual behaviour of scorpionflies, in which the male may gain sex from the female either by presenting a gift of food during court-ship (in which case the female submits voluntarily) or without a nuptial offering, in which case force is necessary to restrain her. The forced copulation is not an abnormal kind of behaviour but is an alternative strategy for gaining sex used more often when there is a shortage of food in the environment to use for gifts.

Socio-biologists propose that human rape appears not as an aberration but as an alternative gene-promotion strategy that is most likely to be adopted by the 'losers' in the competitive, harem-building struggle. If the means of access to legitimate, consenting sex is not available, than a male may be faced with the choice between force or genetic extinction. If he can succeed in impregnating one or two 'stolen' women before being castrated or lynched by the 'owner' males, then his genes (and thus behavioural tendencies) will have been passed on to the next generation of males.

Of course, none of this 'genetic logic' is conscious, nor does it constitute moral justification for rape, but the evolutionary theory does provide a deeper understanding of the phenomenon. Most obviously it explains why rape is an almost exclusively male crime – there is a gross imbalance regarding the commodity value of sexual services for men and women respectively. Secondly, it is consistent with the characteristics of typical rapists – young, virile, high in sex drive, lacking in impulse control, low on the social ladder and likely to have a history of burglary. Thirdly, this theory predicts the characteristics of the typical victim – young, sexually attractive, fertile and vulnerable.

The possibility that rapists are able successfully to evaluate fertility in potential victims is suggested by the finding that women who have been raped are unusually likely to get pregnant as a result (Parkes, 1976). It is also increasingly recognized that if a woman looks like she will put up considerable resistance, most rapists will move on to easier prey, rather in the same manner that a car thief steals cars that are easy to break into. This fact is predictable on the basis of evolutionary theory but rather hard to account for in terms of the 'hatred' theory.

An interesting idea about the evolution of human rape has been put forward by Alexander and Noonan (1979). These authors note that although some anthropologists like Desmond Morris talk about extended receptivity in the human female compared with other primates, it is really more true to describe women as continuously 'non-receptive'. In order to support their strategy of selective mate choice and long-term intimate bonding with particular men, they have evolved a concealed time of ovulation in a form that is like a permanent non-heat. The effect of this is not only to distribute copulations across the cycle, thus promoting bonding and marriage, but also, unfortunately, to encourage pirate copulations – or rape. Since a woman's receptiveness is not highly correlated with ovulation (fertility), there is less reason for the human male to restrict mating to receptive, consenting females. Non-receptive women can still get pregnant, so their protests are, genetically speaking, irrelevant.

Alexander and Noonan note that in many societies rape occurs quite frequently. The women usually submit in order to avoid being hurt and they seldom complain later, perhaps for fear of disrupting the bond with their cuckolded mate. Such rapes appear 'normal', in that they are not especially associated with psychopathology or murder, and the authors suggest that connections of this kind may arise in our society because of the severe penalties attached to rape. Rapists in modern Western society are more likely to be outlaws; moreover they may murder their victim to avoid identification and punishment.

Western society seems to be emerging from a phase in which a great number of rapes went unreported, and a woman's right not to be 'taken' against her will is increasingly recognized. Sociobiology suggests that rape is primarily motivated by sexual disadvantage and deprivation, that women do find it an extremely distasteful, indeed shattering experience and that deterrants in the form of improved detection and heavier penalties are more likely to be effective against rape than appeals to social values or random propaganda directed at the male sex as a whole.

Conclusion

Crime is another area of life in which the behaviour of men and women differs markedly. The kind of aggression that prompts men to fight for territory and advancement of social power seems to be at the root of much violent crime – and probably also war. But other instincts are involved in criminal behaviour, and some of them, such as nest-building, protection of the brood and obsessive jealousy, may in exceptional circumstances lead women into crimes of their own. The time will never come, however, when female rates for armed robbery and burglary equal those of men. Men are by nature nastier animals than women.

8 · *Social Forces and the Sex War*

From the evidence reviewed in previous chapters it is clear that men and women are very different in nature. They have differing and to some extent incompatible interests in the sphere of love and sexual behaviour. They are also different in temperament and motivation and have differing intellectual capacities and modes of thinking. The role of biology seems undeniable. To what extent are social factors also important?

I think there is copious evidence that social learning experiences have power to modify our behaviour, so that we are not in any sense victims of our biological heritage. However, what I contest is the frequent assertion, or even assumption, that social pressure is unidirectional – always operating so as to maximize or enhance natural differences and tendencies. Social forces go both ways.

The case of permissiveness

Consider the range of permissiveness that is seen in the world today. From subscribers of *Forum* to supporters of the 'Festival of Light' there is a great deal of variation within modern society about what is acceptable in sexual behaviour and what is not. Likewise, entire societies show variation with respect to sexual permissiveness (Broude, 1976). There is an enormous gulf between Victorian attitudes and those of modern Europe, and there are vast differences between, for example, San Francisco and Tehran in the extent to which recreational sex is tolerated. This shows that humans are free to arrange their sexual affairs in many different ways. What it does not mean is that heterosexual behaviour is devoid of any biological underpinning.

If Martian sociologists had observed Cambodia during the height of the Khmer Rouge regime, when mere flirting might incur the death penalty, they could easily have concluded that young men have no sex drive. But they would be wrong; the sex drive of Cambodian men would have been just as powerful as that of men anywhere else; only its manifestation would have been suppressed. Society does not alter basic instincts; it just modifies their outward expression.

While societies frequently have norms which prohibit or inhibit various forms of sexual behaviour to which individuals are biologically predisposed, social pressures which promote sexual activity also exist. Pornographic films, sex manuals, peer pressures and special subcultures like 'swinging clubs' and the 'gay set' sometimes encourage sexual behaviour that might not otherwise occur. How many people, after reading the *Kinsey Report*, *The Joy of Sex* or *Fear of Flying*, must have wondered whether they were getting everything they could out of their sex life and sought to extend it in some way? Similarly, there are many people who think that providing sex education in schools and making contraceptives available to young people acts as an incentive to premature and promiscuous sexual escapades. Without wishing to evaluate that particular issue, it does seem that social forces could be, and almost certainly are, deployed to encourage sexual pursuits as well as to discourage them.

Actually, we may question how powerful social forces are when pitted against fundamental biological drives. There is concern, for example, that homosexual foster-parents or teachers are a threat to the normal development of young children in their care. However, the best research evidence available suggests that such fears are largely unfounded.

In a certain Melanesian society called the Sambia young boys are taught as a matter of course to fellate older boys in order to gain the masculinity provided by their semen (Stoller, 1985). This is the only sexual experience that is socially condoned in teenage boys – either fellating older boys or being fellated by younger ones. Social learning theorists would suppose that this experience should result in near universal homosexuality in Sambia men, yet upon reaching adulthood they nearly all marry and slip into heterosexual functioning without any difficulty. The proportion of 'fixated' homosexual men appears to be no higher (or lower) than anywhere else in the world.

Observations such as this show just how difficult it is to alter basic sexual instincts by adjustment of social pressures. Even this most extraordinary intervention does not seem to influence sex orientation, and as we have seen in Chapter 4, male–female differences are equally resilient.

Two myths about sex differences

In the matter of gender differences, social learning theorists usually stress the mechanism by which sexual stereotypes (observations of typical male and female behaviour) are presumed to consolidate the differences in an inflexible kind of way, or even set in motion a spiralling increase in the basic differences. There is every reason to suppose that this may have happened in some cultural contexts, Victorian Europe for example. In 1886, the influential psychiatrist R. Von Krafft-Ebing wrote in his classic book on sexual perversion, *Psychopathia Sexualis:* 'Woman . . . if physically and mentally normal, and properly educated, has but little sexual desire. If it were otherwise, marriage and family would be empty words. As yet the man who avoids women, and the woman who seeks men are sheer anomalies.'

Although relating to a basic truth about gender differences, this statement sounds over-simplified and excessively rigid to the modern ear and is the kind of writing that might lead to social amplification of biological differences.

Similarly, in the educational and occupational spheres, there is no doubt that female opportunities have been severely restricted and a great deal of talent wasted as a result. Many women have undoubtedly suffered injustice in the past because of the social myth that the psychological characteristics and abilities of men and women are totally discrete and that all members of each gender have a God-given duty to perform their assigned role without question.

One of the most outstanding, and outrageous, statements of this point of view is that of the eighteenth-century French philosopher Jean-Jacques Rousseau, who maintained that 'The whole education of women ought to be relative to men. To please them, to be useful to them, to make themselves loved and honoured by them, to educate them when young, to care for them when grown, to counsel them, to console them, and to make life sweet and agreeable to them – these are the duties of women at all times and what should be taught them from their infancy.'

This is an extreme statement, but echoes of it are still heard today. Rigid stereotypes regarding what is, and what can never be, the male and female roles abound in everyday life as well as literature and entertainment. If gender roles were entirely absorbed from the media and attitudes of men and women in the street there is no doubt that even today they could still develop along traditional lines.

More recently, however, the myth of non-overlapping traits and abilities has begun to be rivalled by another – that of psychological identity. According to this equally over-simplified position, men and women are identical by nature and all the traditional differences in their behaviour are due to male-dominated social role learning. Proponents of this new myth appear to favour a policy of reverse discrimination and enforced equality until the roles of men and women merge completely. Thus, for example, we have seen academic institutions in the United States threatened with grant withdrawal unless they increase the proportion of female to male faculty members, leading to a situation in which female academics are less qualified and less productive than men at equivalent levels of status and salary (Over, 1982; Cole and Zuckerman, 1987).

Guidelines issued to authors by major American textbook publishers suggest that inconvenient realities should be suppressed and that the emphasis should be on what *could be* achieved in terms of sexual equality rather than what *is*. The New York Supreme Court has compelled all-male clubs to desegregate while leaving all-female clubs alone. In New Jersey sex discrimination laws were used to compel a football team to admit girls but allowed a hockey team to exclude boys. These and other instances, most obviously with respect to divorce settlements, illustrate the fact that in modern America sex discrimination is acceptable only so long as it is men who are being discriminated against (Levin, 1988).

Totalitarian interference with the language, reminiscent of the way in which the Soviet Union used to rewrite history books every so often, is also seen in many parts of the European world. The New Zealand Broadcasting Corporation appointed a woman as director-general, who proceeded to issue a five-page list of banned, 'sexist' words. These include snowman, actress, manhole, spokeswoman, fisherman, landlord, maiden voyage, mother nature, one-man show, dancing girl, fatherland, chairman, hen party and girl Friday. A few years ago this sort of thing was a joke; now it is really happening. Given that languages normally evolve spontaneously as a reflection of the way people think, such manipulation of the language is nothing short of an attempt to alter the way people think. There are many feminists who would admit this and applaud the development.

In Britain, there is an Equal Opportunities Commission with 'powers to investigate what is taught in schools and make enforceable rulings on them, a power that even the Department of Education does not have' (*Daily Telegraph*, 20 November 1979). As a first use of these powers, 'schools are being told that they may not use reading books with Mummy in the kitchen and Daddy in the garden shed'.

In a letter of protest following the above report, a correspondent to the newspaper, Alan Bradley, wrote:

Book burning is book burning, whether practised by the Nazis in the thirties or the sexists in the seventies. . . . Moreover, it is incontestably true that in the great majority of households which possess both a kitchen and a garden shed, it is Mummy who will normally be found in the former and

Daddy in the latter. To employ the machinery of state to deny the truth is a concept we nowadays call Orwellian. Yet not even that clairvoyant man perceived that in 1984 it would be Big Sister who would be watching us.

Whether one regards this man's reaction as realistic or paranoid, there can be no doubt that the provisions of the Sex Discrimination Act entail various pressures towards the elimination of sex differences. Such pressures may not yet have reached the point where they completely offset the pressures to conform to sexual stereotypes; there is no easy way to compare the relative strengths of these opposing social forces. The point is that although the importance of social learning is undeniable, environmentalists should take account of *all* available models and propaganda – not just those aspects that reinforce nature.

Various messages and exhortations are available in society. What is interesting is why we tune our ear to some and not others. Little boys may learn that some people expect them to fight and be promiscuous, but they are unlikely to be told this at home, school or church. Parents, teachers and churchmen usually try to persuade them to the contrary. Similarly, few parents tell their daughters they must be nurses rather than doctors, secretaries rather then entrepreneurs, and that orgasm is unladylike.

Gender differences may be enhanced or diminished by social and political arrangements; we do not know which of these two tendencies is currently the more powerful. All we can be sure of is that men and women differ in nature to such a degree that it is virtually impossible to override all the differences by social programming. The kibbutz experience and the transformation of women's liberation into feminism in recent years have confirmed this. Heavy-handed attempts to do so are likely not only to fail but to increase the sum total of human unhappiness. The 'androgyny' goal can easily become a new and equally repressive stereotype.

Women and work

Many sociologists have argued that men and women would have similar careers were it not for discrimination in employment and promotion (e.g. Reskin, 1982). Affirmative action programmes have been instituted throughout the Western world in an attempt to enforce integration in the workplace and psychometric tests which show group differences are being banned in many places. The underlying assumption of these programmes is that employers have in the past forced women into menial, low-paid positions and that society conditions everybody to think that this is a natural state of affairs.

Work segregation is sometimes quantified in terms of the proportion of people who would have to change jobs to ensure that all occupations were fully integrated (e.g. men becoming nurses, women becoming bulldozer drivers, etc.). In the United States, the estimate was 68 per cent in 1972, falling to 61 per cent in 1981. Thus there has been some integration in recent years but a considerable imbalance remains and there seems little likelihood of total integration in the foreseeable future.

There are certain problems with the assumption of sexism as an explanation for occupational segregation. One is quite simply economic. The United States is a very competitive market economy, and if women really were available to produce equal output at bargain rates they would surely be in such demand that their premium would rise and wipe out the bargain (Herrnstein, 1985).

Discrimination against women might be attributed to their part-time approach to work (e.g. frequent absences due to child-raising and other responsibilities), hence feminist pressure to have crèches provided at the workplace and to give men paternity leave that would handicap them to a comparable degree. However, the authors in Reskin's book fail to find any evidence to support this hypothesis. For example, women with discontinuous careers were no more likely than other women to end up in segregated jobs.

The authors of the book actually succeed in discarding all environmental theories of sex segregation in the workplace by careful assembly of data and end by acknowledging that they are unable to explain the phenomenon. As Herrnstein (1985) notes, 'they apparently prefer this explanatory vacuum to an obvious alternative' (innate differences between men and women causing them to gravitate towards different jobs).

Herrnstein lists the various areas in which research has shown men and women differ (body strength, motor and perceptual ability, intellectual specialization, temperament, values, etc.) and notes that, even though these differences are minor, with considerable overlap between the sexes, they could translate into major differences in occupational patterns without unfair discrimination being involved. Suppose, for example, that a job had five qualifications, each of which could be met by 60 per cent of men and 40 per cent of woman. An unbiased employer who successfully screened out applicants failing to meet each qualification would end up with a labour force that was eight to one male (because $0 \cdot 6^5$ is about eight times $0 \cdot 4^5$).

Herrnstein supposes that technology will reduce certain occupational differences between men and women (especially those based on strength) and that the intellectual differences may also prove to be unimportant. However, he doubts that the differences in personality and motivation will ever be irrelevant and concludes that, in any case, 'it is surely unscientific to assume as an article of faith that sex segregation in the workplace is entirely unnatural'.

Women and power

Apart from integrating occupational types, there is much concern about the ability of women to climb the promotion ladder within a particular profession. Women have been admitted in large numbers to previously male professions such as medicine and law, but they still have difficulty in competing with men for top posts. For example, in Britain 50 per cent of newly qualified doctors are women, but only about 13 per cent of hospital consultants. Women also gravitate towards the more feminine branches of medicine, such as child psychiatry and community medicine, which usually carry less prestige.

Although many women have stepped on the lower rungs of the political ladder, their representation becomes narrower as they go up, and few reach the top under their own steam. There are virtually no women in the American Senate, the Soviet Politburo or the British Cabinet. Most of the women who have become national leaders effectively inherited the position from husbands or other dynastic connections (compare the award of Nobel prizes, discussed in Chapter 6). For example, Benazir Bhutto of Pakistan, Indira Ghandi of India, Cory Aquino of the Philippines and Evita Peron of Argentina all gained power after the death of a charismatic male with whom they were closely associated. Their supporters were no doubt trying to extend the influence of the deceased by vicarious charisma, thus maintaining the unity and stability of the country. Margaret Thatcher is a notable exception to this pattern.

These facts do not answer the question of whether differential promotion reflects a natural state of affairs or a sexist bias. They do, however, indicate that feminism has so far made limited progress in reorganizing the social power structure. The male drive to achieve is not easy to compete with and even when the top is reached some women are ambivalent about their success.

The head of the British Equal Opportunities Commission, Joanna Foster, was quoted as saying: 'American women climbed up the career ladder fast; but when they got to the boardroom they looked around and saw that all the men had pictures of their families on their desks. The women didn't have any pictures of their families. They didn't have any families . . . so if British employers want to keep women, they will have to consider the family too.'

Different interests

A major reason why men and women gravitate towards different occupations seems to be that of interest. Men seem naturally more intrigued by abstract ideas, mechanics and science, as well as personal success and power, and women

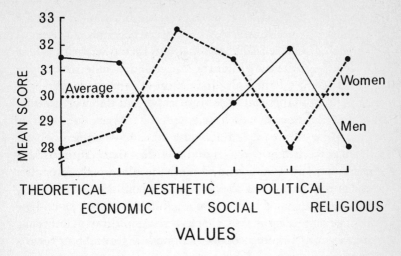

Figure 12 Differences between men and women in a survey of personal values (from Allport and Vernon, 1931).

appear to be more interested in art, religion, child development and interpersonal relationships. This is seen in direct surveys of value priority (see Figure 12), choices of reading material (for instance, science fiction as opposed to romantic novels) and television viewing preferences (westerns as opposed to soap operas).

These interests carry through into educational specializations. For example, of bachelors degrees awarded in the United States in 1979, the following percentages were awarded to women (Randour, Strasburg and Lipman-Blumen, 1982): literature and library science, 80 per cent; education, 68 per cent; mathematics, 34 per cent; physical science and computers, 18 per cent; and engineering, 6 per cent. Much the same pattern is observed in Britain. Although there are more women in higher education overall today than there were a few decades ago, the pattern of subject preferences has remained much the same.

It has sometimes been argued that women avoid mathematics because they lack confidence in their ability or because they have 'learned to be helpless' in this regard. However, studies specifically designed to untangle the different possible reasons for educational choice point to the overwhelming importance of the incentive value attached to the various subject areas (Eccles, Adler and Meece, 1984). Men apparently do well in mathematics and science because although, like women, they see these subjects as more difficult than English, they also perceive achievement in these areas as more important and worth while. Women are not so much frightened of these subjects, or anticipating failure (as some psychologists have argued), as less convinced that mathematics and science would be rewarding endeavours. Thus interest and motivation are probably more important than ability, opportunity, or confidence.

Probably a major reason women find the pursuit of mathematics unappealing is that it lacks human interest. Women are generally much more people-orientated. If they do not have a family of their own, they often prefer to work as teachers, nurses, receptionists, counsellors, entertainers, etc. – occupations in which they can talk with people and perhaps help them. This is not just social conditioning; it is very much part of the nature of most women.

Female truth

Apart from different interests, it seems that women operate with a rather different belief system from men. While men value logic and empirical fact, women often prefer mystical, magical views of life and the world. For example, in a survey I conducted of over four thousand ordinary British adults, women emerged as much more superstitious and religious than men. Thirty-nine per cent of women believed in astrology, compared with 22 per cent of men, 18 per cent of women believed in palm-reading, as opposed to 7 per cent of men, and 42 per cent of women believed in life after death, compared with 29 per cent of men. On the other hand, more men than women believed in UFOs (30 per cent as opposed to 26 per cent of women). As in many aspects of life, men and women often seem to think differently.

As more women enter the social sciences, there are signs of

pressure towards redefining the concept of truth in female favour. In a recent book called *Feminism and Freedom*, New York philosopher Michael Levin (1988) argues that many feminists begin by evading the evidence of innate and profound male–female differences and then proceed to deny the concept of truth itself. He quotes feminist academics as follows:

> 'Truth, reality and objectivity are all in trouble from our point of view; we see a male-created truth, a male point of view, a male-defined objectivity.' (Ruth Bleier in *Science and Gender*)
> 'The postulate of value-free research, of neutrality and indifference towards the research objects, has to be replaced by conscious partiality. . . .' (Renate Klein)
> 'Feminism withdraws from the patriarchal construction of reality.' (Blanche Dubois)

Levin gives many other examples of the feminist argument that scientific truth as we once knew it must give way to new female-centred modes of thinking, in which objective facts are treated as less important than intuition, values and political ends.

This particular feminist touch is less intrusive in the 'soft sciences', which have always had advocates of 'humanism', than in the physical sciences, which need to be more exact. The female mode of thinking is not optimal for putting a spacecraft on Mars, however much it may help us 'feel good about it' once we have done it.

Which sex is superior?

Evolutionary theorists are sometimes accused of saying that men are superior to women. Indeed, Darwin himself did make statements to that effect. However, this makes no sense. Superiority cannot be assessed in the abstract – it must always be related to some measurable attribute. We have seen that men are superior to women as regards certain traits, such as strength and spatial reasoning, but women are superior to men as regards other qualities, such as physical endurance, empathy and verbal intelligence. As far as height, libido and ambitiousness are concerned, there are clear differences between the sexes, but it is hard to say which end of the scale is preferable, so the concept of superiority is irrelevant. Neither sex is superior in general, but each has qualities that are beneficial to the species and society, as well as being important for the genetic survival of the individual member of that gender.

Lest anyone should imagine I have a bias towards attributing favourable characteristics to my own gender, I readily admit that the male constitution is responsible for the vast majority of social problems. The cool, aggressive masculinity that makes the average man better at bomb disposal than the average woman *in extremis* leads to psychopathy and violent criminality. Female equivalents of the 'Yorkshire Ripper' and 'Son of Sam' are very rare indeed. Likewise, male lust, ambition and territorialism, although they confer reproductive fitness to the individuals concerned, are probably at the root of most rapes, muggings, assassinations and even wars. With present levels of violence in society, the female qualities of empathy and nurturance are very much at a premium. Even the male tendency towards polygamy is more socially disruptive than the female inclination towards monogamy. The former leads to discontent, conflict, jealousy and sometimes even bloodshed, while the latter promotes equity and harmony. Altogether, it is probably fair to say that women are morally superior to men. It is not hard to see why many feminists dislike men and refer to them as 'pigs'.

This highlights a very important point that was touched upon earlier – the need to separate scientific arguments from those that are moral and political. I have presented evidence that males are naturally more sexually adventurous and aggressive than women, but this should not be interpreted as an endorsement or justification of such behaviour. Nor am I saying that promiscuity and war are inevitable because of these instinctual male tendencies. In fact, I believe that society has both the power and the duty to curtail the more base of our animal instincts. This end, however, will best be achieved by recognition of what we have to contend with in human nature rather than an ostrich-like refusal to acknowledge it.

With respect to sex differences in the educational and occupational spheres, I personally feel that rather more equality of treatment and opportunity than we have so far attained is desirable. Women have been treated abominably in the past, and still are in many parts of the world. Even in modern European society, various forms of discrimination against women are rife. However, in drawing up plans for a campaign to eliminate such injustices, the feminist movement would be well advised to work within a framework that is explicitly moral and political rather than base arguments on fallible scientific assertions about biological equivalence.

If the case for equality of treatment is made to rest upon an assumption of psychological identity, it will run the risk of rejection because of scientific disproof. Equal we may be, but identical we are not. Far better to concede the average biological differences but to emphasize that the overlap between men and women is so great, particularly in the area of intellectual capacities, that there can be no justification, moral or scientific, for treating people as anything other than individuals.

References

Alexander, R.D. and Noonan, K.M. Concealment of ovulation, parental care and human social evolution. In: N.A. Chagnon and W. Irons (eds) *Evolutionary Biology and Human Social Behaviour*. North Scituate, Mass.: Duxbury Press, 1979.

Allport, G.W. and Vernon, P.E. A test for personal values. *Journal of Abnormal Psychology*, 1931, 26, 231–48.

Antonovsky, H.F. *Adolescent Sexuality*. Lexington: D.C. Heath, 1980.

Bancroft, J., The control of deviant sexual behaviour by drugs. *Journal of International Medical Research*, 1975, 3, 20–21.

—— Sexual desire and the brain. *Sexual and Marital Therapy*, 1988, 3, 11–27.

Bandura, A. *Social Learning Theory*. Englewood Cliffs, NJ: Prentice Hall, 1977.

Bardis, P.D. Homeric Love. In: M. Cook and G.D. Wilson (eds) *Love and Attraction: An International Conference*. Oxford: Pergamon, 1979.

Bardwick, J.M. *Psychology of Women: A Study of Biocultural Conflicts*. New York: Harper and Row, 1971.

Beamer, W., Berman, G. and Clegg, M. Copulatory behaviour of the ram, Ovis Aires II: factors affecting copulatory satiation. *Animal Behaviour*, 1969, 17, 706–11.

Bell, A.P. Homosexualities: their range and character. *Nebraska Symposium on Motivation*. Lincoln: University of Nebraska Press, 1973.

——, Weinberg, M.S. and Hammersmith, S.K. *Sexual Preference: Its Development in Men and Women*. Bloomington: Indiana University Press, 1981.

Bermant, G. Sexual behaviour: hard times with the Coolidge Effect. In: M.H. Siegel and H.P. Zeigler (eds) *Psychological Research: The Inside Story*. New York: Harper and Row, 1976.

—— and Davidson, J.M. *Biological Basis of Sexual Behaviour*. New York: Harper and Row, 1974.

147

Berry, A. Animal skinheads. *Daily Telegraph*, 3 October 1983.

Berry, C. The Nobel scientists and the origins of scientific achievement. *British Journal of Sociology*, 1981, 32, 381–91.

Blumstein, P.W. and Schwartz, P. Bisexuality: some social psychological issues. *Journal of Social Issues*, 1977, 33, 30–45.

Boudouris, J. Homicide and the family. *Journal of Marriage and the Family*, 1971, 33, 667–76.

Broude, G.J. Cross-cultural patterning of some sexual attitudes and practices. *Behaviour Science Research*, 1976, 11, 227–62.

Brownmiller, S. *Against Our Will: Men, Women and Rape*. New York, Bantam Books, 1975.

Buffery, A.H. and Gray, J.A. Sex differences in the development of spatial and linguistic skills. In: C. Ounsted and D.C. Taylor (eds) *Gender Differences: Their Ontology and Significance*. London: Churchill Livingstone, 1972.

Carney, A., Bancroft, J. and Mathews, A. Combination of hormonal and psychological treatment for female sexual unresponsiveness. *British Journal of Psychiatry*, 1978, 132, 339–46.

Christensen, H.T. and Gregg, C.F. Changing sex norms in America and Scandinavia. *Journal of Marriage and the Family*, 1970, 32, 616–27.

Cole, J.R. and Zuckerman, H. Marriage, motherhood and research performance in science. *Scientific American*, 1987, 225, 119–25.

Coltheart, M., Hull, E. and Slater, D. Sex differences in imagery and reading. *Nature*, 1975, 253, 437–40.

Curran, J.P. Convergence toward a single sexual standard? *Social Behaviour and Personality*, 1975, 3, 189–95.

Dabbs, J.M., Frady, R.L., Carr, T.S. and Besch, N.F. Saliva testosterone and criminal violence in young adult prison inmates. *Psychological Medicine*, 1987, 49, 174–82.

Dabbs, J.M., Ruback, R.B., Frady, R.L., Hopper, C.H. and Sgoutas, D.S. Saliva testosterone and criminal violence among women. *Personality and Individual Differences*, 1988, 9, 269–75.

Daly, M. and Wilson, M. Sex and strategy. *New Scientist*, 4 January 1979, 15–17.

—— Evolutionary psychology and family violence. In: C. Crawford, M. Smith and D. Krebs (eds) *Sociobiology and Psychology: Ideas, Issues and Applications*. Hillsdale, NJ, Erlbaum Associates, 1987.

Darwin, C.R. *The Descent of Man and Selection in Relation to Sex*. London: John Murray (revised edn), 1881.

Dawkins, R. *The Selfish Gene*. Oxford: Oxford University Press, 1976.

Dawson, J.L.M. Effects of sex hormones on cognitive style in rats and men. *Behaviour Genetics*, 1972, 2, 21–41.

D'Orban, P.T. and Dalton, K. Violent crime and the menstrual cycle. *Psychological Medicine*, 1980, 10, 353–9.

Dorner, G. *Hormones and Brain Differentiation*. Amsterdam: Elsevier, 1976.

Eccles, J., Adler, T. and Meece, J.L. Sex differences in achievement: a test of alternate theories. *Journal of Personality and Social Psychology*, 1984 46, 26–43.

Eibl-Eibesfeldt, I. *Love and Hate: On the Natural History of Basic Behaviour Patterns*. London: Methuen, 1971.

Elias, M. Serum cortisol, testosterone, and testosterone-binding globulin responses to competitive fighting in human males. *Aggressive Behaviour*, 1981, 7, 215–24.

Ellis, L. Evidence of neuroandrogenic etiology of sex roles from a combined analysis of human, non-human primate and non-primate mammalian studies. *Personality and Individual Differences*, 1986, 7, 519–52.

—— and Ames, M.A. Neurohormonal functioning and sexual orientation: a theory of homosexuality–heterosexuality. *Psychological Bulletin*, 1987, 101, 233–58.

Epstein, A.W. The phylogenetics of fetishism. In: G.D. Wilson (ed.) *Variant Sexuality: Research and Theory*. London: Croom Helm, 1987.

Eysenck, H.J. *Sex and Personality*. London: Open Books, 1976.

—— and Wilson, G.D. *A Textbook of Human Psychology*, Lancaster: Medical and Technical Publishers Press, 1976.

Feldman, M.P. and MacCullough, M.J. *Homosexual Behaviour: Therapy and Assessment*, New York: Pergamon, 1971.

Fisher, S. *Understanding the Female Orgasm*. Harmondsworth: Penguin, 1973.

Flor-Henry, P. Cerebral aspects of sexual deviation. In: G.D. Wilson (ed.) *Variant Sexuality: Research and Theory*. London: Croom Helm, 1987.

Ford, C.S. and Beach, F.A. *Patterns of Sexual Behaviour*, New York: Harper and Row, 1951.

Freedman, D.G. *Human Sociobiology: A Holistic Approach*. New York: Free Press, 1979.

Freeman, D. *Margaret Mead and Samoa: The Making and Unmaking of an Anthropological Myth*. Cambridge, Mass.: Harvard University Press, 1983.

Fremlin, J.H. The evolution of God. *New Humanist*, March 1974, 377-8.

Friedan, B. *The Second Stage*. London: Michael Joseph, 1982.

Frodi, A., Macaulay, J. and Thorne, P.R. Are women always less aggressive than men? A review of the literature. *Psychological Bulletin*, 1977, 84, 634-60.

Gallup, G.G. Unique features of human sexuality in the context of evolution. In: D. Byrne and K. Kelley (eds) *Alternative Approaches to the Study of Sexual Behaviour*, Hillsdale, NJ: Erlbaum Associates, 1986.

Geist, V. *Mountain Sheep: A Study in Behavior and Evolution*. Chicago: University of Chicago Press, 1971.

Giallombardo, R. *The Social World of Imprisoned Girls*. New York: Wiley, 1974.

Gillan, P. and Gillan, R. *Sex Therapy Today* London: Open Books, 1976.

Gladue, B.A., Green, R. and Hellman, R.E. Neuroendocrine response to oestrogen and sexual orientation. *Science*, 1984, 225, 1496-9.

Goldberg, S. *The Inevitability of Patriarchy*. London: Temple Smith, 1977.

—— and Lewis, M. Play behaviour in the year-old infant: early sex differences. *Child Development*, 1969, 40, 21-31.

Goodall, J. *In the Shadow of Man*, New York: Dell, 1971.

Gosselin, C.C. and Eysenck, S.B.G. The transvestite double image: a preliminary report. *Personality and Individual Differences*, 1980, 1, 172-3.

Gosselin, C.C. and Wilson, G.D. *Sexual Variations: Fetishism, Transvestism and Sadomasochism*. London: Faber and Faber, 1980.

Greenblat, R.B. Joan of Arc: syndrome of feminizing testes. *British Journal Of Sexual Medicine*, 1981, August, 54.

Griffitt, W. and Hatfield, E. *Human Sexual Behaviour*. London: Scott Foresman and Co., 1985.

Halpern, D.F. *Sex Differences in Cognitive Abilities*, Hillsdale, NJ: Erlbaum Associates, 1986.

Harcourt, A.H. and Stewart, K.J. Apes, sex and societies. *New Scientist*, 20 October 1977, 160-62.

Harlow, H.F. Sexual behaviour in the Rhesus monkey. In: F.A. Beach (ed.) *Sex and Behaviour*. New York: Wiley, 1965.

Harris, L.J. Sex differences in spatial ability. In: M. Kinsbourne (ed.) *Assymetrical Function of the Brain*. Cambridge: Cambridge University Press, 1978.

Hart, B.L. Gonadal androgen and sociosexual behaviour of male mammals: a comparative analysis. *Psychological Bulletin*, 1974, 81, 383–400.

Harter, S. Mastery, motivation and the need for approval in older children and their relationship to social desirability response tendencies. *Developmental Psychology*, 1975, 11, 186–96.

Herrnstein, R.J. Are women workers different? *Fortune*, 1 April 1985.

Hill, D. Depression: disease, reaction, or posture? *American Journal of Psychiatry*, 1968, 125, 445.

Hite, S. *The Hite Report*. New York: Macmillan, 1976.

Howard, R., Gifford, M. and Lumsden, J. Changes in an electrocortical measure of impulsivity during the menstrual cycle. *Personality and Individual Differences*, 1988, 9, 917–18.

Hyde, J.S. How large are cognitive gender differences? A meta-analysis using W^2 and d. *American Psychologist*, 1981, 36, 892–901.

Imperato-McGinley, J., Guerrero, L., Gautier, T. and Peterson, R.E. Steroid 5-alpha-reductase deficiency in man: an inherited form of male pseudohermaphoditism. *Science*, 1974, 186, 1213–15.

Iwawaki, S. and Wilson, G.D. Sex fantasies in Japan. *Personality and Individual Differences*, 1983, 4, 543–5.

Kallmann, F.J. Comparative twin study of the genetic aspects of male homosexuality. *Journal of Nervous and Mental Diseases*, 1952, 115, 283.

Kamel, G.W.L. Leather sex: Meaningful aspects of gay sadomasochism. *Deviant Behaviour*, 1980, 1, 171–91.

Kane, F.J., Lipton, M.A. and Ewing, J.A. Hormonal influences in female sexual response. *Archives of General Psychiatry*, 1969, 20, 202–9.

Kaplan, H.S. *The New Sex Therapy*, Vol. II: *Disorders of Sexual Desire and Other New Concepts and Techniques in Sex Therapy*. New York: Brunner/Mazel, 1979.

Karlsson, J.L. Genetic association of giftedness and creativity with schizophrenia. *Hereditas*, 1970, 66, 177–82.

Katchadourian, H.A. and Lunde, D.T. *Fundamentals of Human Sexuality*. New York: Holt, Rinehart and Winston, 1975.

King, K., Balswick, J.O. and Robinson, I.E. The continuing premarital sexual revolution among college females. *Journal of Marriage and the Family*, 1977, 39, 455–9.

Kolb, B. and Whishaw, I.Q. *Fundamentals of Human Neuropsychology* (2nd edn). New York: Freeman, 1985.

Krafft-Ebing, R. *Psychopathia Sexualis* (12th edn), 1886. Translated by F.S. Klaf. New York: Stein and Day, 1965.

La Torre, R.A. Devaluation of the human love object: heterosexual rejection as a possible antecedent to fetishism. *Journal of Abnormal Psychology*, 1980, 89, 295–8.

Lehrke, R.G. Sex linkage: a biological basis for greater male variability in intelligence. In: R.T. Osborne, C.E. Noble and N. Weyl (eds) *Human Variations: The Biopsychology of Age, Race and Sex*. New York, Academic Press, 1978.

Leonard, E.B. *Women, Crime and Society*. New York: Longman, 1982.

Levin, M. *Feminism and Freedom*. New York: Transaction Press, 1988.

Loney, J. Background factors, sexual experiences and attitudes towards treatment in two 'normal' homosexual samples. *Journal of Consulting and Clinical Psychology*, 1974, 38, 57–65.

Maccoby, E.E. and Jacklin, C.N. *The Psychology of Sex Differences*. Stanford, CA: Stanford University Press, 1974.

Maclean, P.D. Sensory and perceptive factors in emotional functions of the triune brain. In: L. Levi (ed.) *Emotions: Their Parameters and Measurement*. New York: Raven Press, 1975.

McGlone, J. Sex differences in human brain assymetry: a critical survey. *Behavioural and Brain Sciences*, 1980, 3, 215–63.

McGuire, M.T., Raleigh, M.J. and Johnson, C. Social dominance in adult male vervet monkeys: behaviour-biochemical relationships. *Biology and Social Life*, 1983, 22, 311–28.

Marshall, S.P. and Smith, J.D. Sex differences in learning mathematics: a longitudinal study with item and error analysis. *Journal of Educational Psychology*, 1987, 4, 372–83.

Mazur, A. and Lamb, T.A. Testosterone, status and mood in human males. *Hormones and Behaviour*, 1980, 14, 236–46.

Mead, M. *Coming of Age in Samoa*. London: Jonathan Cape, 1929.

—— *Sex and Temperament in Three Primitive Societies*. New York: Morrow, 1935.

—— *Male and Female: A Study of the Sexes in a Changing World*. New York: Morrow, 1967.

Meuser, W. and Nieschlag, E. Sexualhormone und stimmlage des mannes. *Deutsch Medizinische Wochenschrift*, 1977, 102, 261.

Meyer-Bahlburg, H.F.L. Sex hormones and female homosexuality: a critical examination. *Archives of Sexual Behaviour*, 1979, 8, 101–19.

Mitchell, G. *Human Sex Differences: A Primatologist's Perspective*. New York: Van Nostrand, 1981.

Moir, A. and Jessell, D. *Brain Sex*. London: Michael Joseph, 1989.

Money, J. Prenatal hormones and post-natal socialization in gender identity differentiation. *Nebraska Symposium on Motivation*. Lincoln: University of Nebraska Press, 1973.

—— and Ehrhardt, A.A. *Man and Woman, Boy and Girl*. Baltimore: Johns Hopkins University Press, 1972.

Morris, D. *Intimate Behaviour*. London: Cape, 1971.

—— *The Human Zoo*. London: Triad/Panther, 1979.

Moulin, L. The Nobel prizes for sciences from 1901–50: an essay in sociological analysis. *British Journal of Sociology*, 1955, 6, 246–63.

Mulder, M.B. The relevance of the polygyny threshold model to humans. In: G.G.N. Mascie-Taylor and A.J. Boyce (eds) *Human Mating Patterns*. Cambridge: Cambridge University Press, 1988.

Murdock, G.P. *Ethnographic Atlas*, Pittsburgh: University of Pittsburgh Press, 1967.

Nadler, R.D. Sexual behaviour of captive orangutans. *Archives of Sexual Behaviour*, 1977, 6, 457–75.

Nicholson, J. *Men and Women: How Different Are They?* Oxford: Oxford University Press, 1984.

Nyborg, G. Spatial ability in men and women: review and new theory. *Advances in Behaviour Research and Therapy*, 1983, 5, 89–140.

Over, R. Research productivity and impact of male and female psychologists. *American Psychologist*, 1982, 37, 24–31.

Parkes, A.S. *Patterns of Sexuality and Reproduction*. London: Oxford University Press, 1976.

Peplau, L.A., Rubin, Z. and Hill, C.T. Sexual intimacy in dating relationships. *Journal of Social Issues*, 1977, 33, 86–109.

Petty, G.M. and Dawson, B. Sexual aggression in normal men: incidence, beliefs and personality characteristics. *Personality and Individual Differences*, 1989, 10, 355–62.

Purifoy, F.E. and Koopmans, L.H. Androstenedione, testosterone, and free testosterone concentration in women of various occupations. *Social Biology*, 1979, 26, 179–88.

Quadagno, D.M., Briscoe, R. and Quadagno, J.S. Effect of perinatal gonadal hormones on selected non-sexual behaviour patterns: a critical assessment of the non-human and human literature. *Psychological Bulletin*, 1977, 84, 62–80.

Randour, M., Strasburg, G. and Lipman-Blumen, J. Women in higher education: trends in enrolment and degrees earned. *Harvard Educational Review*, 1982, 52, 189–202.

Reinisch, J.M. Prenatal exposure of human foetuses to synthetic progestin and oestrogen affects personality. *Nature*, 1977, 266, 246–63.

Reskin, B.F. (ed.) *Sex, Segregation and the Workplace: Trends, Explanations, Remedies*. New York: National Academic Press, 1982.

Rimland, B. *Infantile Autism.* New York: Appleton, Century, Crofts, 1964.

Robertson, D.R. Social control of sex reversal in a coral-reef fish. *Science,* 1972, 177, 1007–9.

Rose, R.M., Bernstein, I.S. and Gordon, T.P. Consequences of social conflict on plasma testosterone levels in Rhesus monkeys. *Psychosomatic Medicine,* 1975, 37, 50–61.

Sanders, G. and Ross-Field, L. Sexual orientation and visuospatial ability. *Brain and Cognition* 1986, 5, 280–90.

Sarri, R.C. Crime and the female offender. In: E.S. Gomberg and V. Franks (eds) *Gender and Disordered Behaviour.* New York: Brunner-Mazel, 1979.

Schindler, G.L. Testosterone concentration, personality patterns and occupational choice in women (doctoral dissertation, University of Houston). *Dissertation Abstracts,* 1979, 4090, 1411A. (University Microfilms No. 79-19403.)

Schlegel, W.S. Parameter Beckenskelett. *Sexualmedizin,* 1975, 4, 228–32.

Seward, J.P. and Seward, G.H. *Sex Differences: Mental and Temperamental.* Lexington: D.C. Heath, 1980.

Sherfey, M.D. *The Nature and Evolution of Female Sexuality.* New York: Random House, 1972.

Shope, D.F. The orgastic responsiveness of selected college females. *Journal of Sex Research,* 1968, 4, 206–19.

Silver, R. and Feder, H.H. (eds) *Hormones and Reproductive Behaviour: Readings from Scientific American.* San Francisco: W.H. Freeman and Co., 1964.

Simonton, D.K. *Scientific Genius: A Psychology of Science.* Cambridge: Cambridge University Press, 1988.

Sipova, I. and Starka, L. Plasma testosterone values in transsexual women. *Archives of Sexual Behaviour,* 1977, 6, 477–81.

Solanis, V. Scum Manifesto (Society for Cutting Up Men). In: R. Morgan (ed.) *Sisterhood Is Powerful.* NY, Random House, 1970.

Spengler, A. Manifest sadomasochism of males: results of an empirical study. *Archives of Sexual Behaviour,* 1977, 6, 441–55.

Spiro, M.E. *Gender and Culture: Kibbutz Women Revisited.* Durham, NC: Duke University Press, 1979.

Stoller, R.J. *Observing the Erotic Imagination.* New Haven: Yale University Press, 1985.

Storie, V.J. Male and female car drivers: differences observed in accidents. *Transport and Road Research Laboratory Report,* no. 761, 1977.

Symons, D. *The Evolution of Human Sexuality*. New York: Oxford University Press, 1979.

—— and Ellis, B. Male–female differences in the desire to have intercourse with an anonymous new partner. In: A. Rasa, C. Vogel and E. Voland (eds) *Sociobiology of Reproductive Strategies in Animals and Humans*. London: Croom Helm, 1988.

Thornhill, R. and Thornhill, N.W. Human rape: the strengths of the evolutionary perspective. In: C. Crawford, M. Smith and D. Krebs (eds) *Sociobiology and Psychology: Ideas, Issues, and Applications*. Hillsdale, NJ: Erlbaum Associates, 1987.

Tiger, L. *Men in Groups*. New York: Random House, 1969.

Trivers, R.L. Parental investment and sexual selection. In: B. Campbell (ed.) *Sexual Selection and the Descent of Man*. Chicago: Aldine, 1972.

—— Sexual selection and resource-accruing abilities in *Anolis Garmani*. *Evolution*, 1976, 30, 253–69.

Udry, J.R. *The Social Context of Marriage* (3rd edn). Philadelphia: Lippincott, 1974.

—— and Morris, N.M. Distribution of coitus in the menstrual cycle. *Nature*, 1968, 220, 593–6.

Wallin, P. A study of orgasm as a condition of women's enjoyment of intercourse. *Journal of Social Psychology*, 1960, 51, 191–8.

Weinreich, H. Sex-role socialisation. In: J. Chetwynd and D. Harnett (eds) *The Sex-Role System*. London: Routledge and Kegan Paul, 1978.

Wikan, U. Man becomes woman: transsexualism in Oman as a key to gender roles. *Man*, 1977, 12, 304–19.

Wilson, G.D. *The Secrets of Sexual Fantasy*. London: Dent, 1978.

—— The sociobiology of sex differences. *Bulletin of the British Psychological Society*, 1979, 32, 350–53.

—— *Love and Instinct*. London: Temple Smith, 1981(a).

—— Cross-generational stability of gender differences in sexuality. *Personality and Individual Differences*, 1981(b), 2, 254–7.

—— Finger length as an index of assertiveness in women. *Personality and Individual Differences*, 1983, 4, 111–12.

—— The personality, of opera singers. *Personality and Individual Differences*, 1984, 5, 195–201.

—— Male–female differences in sexual activity, enjoyment and fantasies. *Personality and Individual Differences*, 1987(a), 8, 125–7.

—— An ethological approach to sexual deviation. In: Wilson, G.D. (ed.) *Variant Sexuality: Research and Theory*. London: Croom Helm, 1987(b).

—— The sociobiological basis of sexual dysfunction. In: M. Cole and W. Dryden (eds) *Sex Therapy in Britain*. Milton Keynes: Open University Press, 1988.

—— and Cox, D.N. *The Child Lovers: A Study of Paedophiles in Society*. London: Peter Owen, 1983.

—— and Iwawaki, S. Social attitudes in Japan. *Journal of Social Psychology*, 1980, 112, 175–80.

—— and Lang, R.J. Sex differences in sexual fantasy patterns. *Personality and Individual Differences*, 1981, 2, 343–6.

—— and Nias, D.K.B. *Love's Mysteries: The Psychology of Sexual Attraction*. London: Open Books, 1976.

—— and Reading, A.E. Pelvic shape, gender role conformity and sexual satisfaction. *Personality and Individual Differences*, 1989, in press.

Zuckerman, S. *The Social Life of Monkeys and Apes*. London: Routledge and Kegan Paul (2nd edn), 1981.

Index